Tamar Valley Pantry

Philip Kuruvita . John T Bailey

4

Published in 2013 by: Philip Kuruvita Photography
18 Upton Street, Launceston, Tasmania 7250
phone: +61 (0)3 63342462
email: mail@kuruvita.com.au
www.kuruvita.com.au

Photography by Philip Kuruvita
Recipes by John T. Bailey except pages 28, 30 and 118
Design by Vicki Kuruvita

Photography copyright: © 2013 Philip Kuruvita

Recipe copyright: © 2013 John T. Bailey
all pages except pg 28, 30 and 118

Design copyright: © 2013 Vicki Kuruvita

All rights reserved. No part of this publication may be reproduced, stored in a retrieval system or transmitted in any form or by any means, electronic, mechanical, photocopying, recording or otherwise, without the prior written permission of the publisher

Printed in China by Everbest Printing Co Ltd

National Library of Australia Cataloguing-in-Publication entry
Author: Kuruvita, Philip, author.
Title: Tamar Valley pantry / Philip Kuruvita ; Vicki Kuruvita ; John T. Bailey.
ISBN: 9780992348502 (hardback)
Notes: Includes index.
Subjects: Gastronomy--Tasmania--Tamar, River, Valley.
Food industry and trade--Tasmania--Tamar, River, Valley.
Tamar, River, Valley (Tas.)--Social life and customs.
Tamar, River, Valley (Tas.)--Description and travel.
Other Authors/Contributors:
Kuruvita, Vicki, author.
Bailey, John T., author.
Dewey Number: 394.109465

Every effort has been made to ensure that the information in this book is accurate at the time of going to press. The publishers cannot accept the responsibility for any errors or omissions

5

contents

7	it's a five recipe friday...
12	food has always been important in our family...
14	many thanks to...
17	suppliers
18	recipes
222	cook's notes
224	kitchen essentials
230	suppliers listing
238	index

it's a five recipe friday...

It's a five recipe Friday, the day I visit chef John T. Bailey in his Cataract Gorge kitchen during the final weeks of preparation for this book. He is charmingly cranky because his scallops and micro salad are late.

On the other (safe) side of the kitchen counter it is all Sri Lankan calm, as photographer Philip Kuruvita adjusts his camera lenses and readies himself for his role in the day's theatre.

They are two Grand Masters – Kuruvita one of only 15 Grand Masters of Photography in Australia and Bailey from the Dorchester Hotel with Anton Mosimann (London) to chef for Kerry Packer at his Kosciusko Alpine resort and finally `resting', like a good piece of Wagyu beef – in the Tamar Valley region of Australia.

Is Bailey's Cataract Gorge kitchen big enough for them both?

Within minutes, the scallops and salad are bounding up the stairs, carried by the providore – who is all bluster and apology. A short and colourful verbal joust follows and before you can say `truffle' Bailey is searing the scallops with a ginger and wasabi butter and arranging them on a bed of buckwheat noodles.

In our neck of the woods – the Tamar Valley region of Northern Tasmania - innovation and climate are the drivers of our super premium food and wine industries.

``What scallops? Whose cheese? Whose truffles? Whose micro salad? AND, who grew that spectacular Sunday roast lamb we enjoyed at your place?''

In the Tamar Valley, our next meal; who grew the food and where can we get 'some' are part of the daily conversation – in the Boardroom – at the local market – at the school gate – we are a region of lovers of great food.

For generations, this fertile river valley has delivered top grade produce. Tamar Valley residents are spoiled like Parisian gourmands. For generations our highly skilled farmers, cheesemakers and fisherman have delivered excellence.

John was one of a very small handful of chefs who identified the region's outward potential 20 years ago when he arrived from London. His understanding of quality and its kitchen potential has been vindicated and is showcased in this book.
"Cooking is a serious business, demanding Holy Devotion! I don't fix cars, build houses, or play the violin, I do food!"

To John, a day without cooking is a day without meaning. "I am the eternal apprentice"

In winter, the misty Tamar River is like an impressionist's canvas and the damp chill calls for steaming pasta tossed in local olive oil and sprinkled with freshly shaved truffle. Summer's ripened figs, berries and the fresh cheeses of autumn beg for a sniffle of Josef Chromy's Ruby Pinot.

Throughout this book Kuruvita has quite sublimely captured the clean summer blue/pink light and landscape against the brash berries in the aperitif of Tasmania's four seasons.

Or, the comforting softness of Tamar Valley winter – where mist and light struggle for supremacy on any given winter morning – winter is our main course.

Whether, like us you live and work in the region, or have visited on holiday, you will find this book answers your Tamar Valley hunger pangs.

John's recipes and Phil's imagery will inspire you to hunt and gather and amaze yourself with how simple great food really can be.

Five times Tasmanian Professional Photographer of the Year, a Fellow of both the Australian and New Zealand Institutes of Professional Photography, Philip is Tasmania's only Grand Master of Photography - one of just 15 in Australia.
"While it is great to win awards and be recognized for the work that you do, for me it is still, after all these years, the thrill of capturing the moment in a way that resonates with people who see my images that gets me up in the morning", he says.

Twenty winters after we first met as émigré to this island state we, the chef, the photographer and the journalist have cooked, photographed and written about almost every morsel this magical place produces.

This book, by Bailey and Kuruvita reflects with great pride the emergence of the Tamar Valley as one of the nation's great food regions.

Danielle Blewett
Tasmanian Journalist and Media Adviser since 1991
Food and Wine editor, The Examiner Newspaper 1993 - 2003

food has always been important in our family...

I guess it is for many families, which is why cookbooks and cooking shows are so popular. There were no rules, but we would sit together for meals whenever we could. Some of my earliest memories are based around being allowed to stay up past my bedtime when Dad was working late and being fed hot spicy rice and curry straight off his plate as he ate with his fingers, the way I still eat curry today.

Being born in England to a Sri Lankan father and an Austrian mother, I never got the chance to be fussy about my food. A mixture of strudels and schnitzels, curries and school dinners (you know, the ones that Jamie Oliver has been waging war on) meant that there was always something different on offer and the chances of getting bored was remote.

Eight years living in Sri Lanka meant that I got to know one of the most flavoursome and subtle cuisine of the world, and our subsequent move to Australia 39 years ago was nothing short of a culture shock.

In the mid 70's Australia had yet to undergo the massive change that would make it one of the most multicultural cuisines on the planet. Back then, the use of garlic or the drinking of red wine was viewed with considerable suspicion, and we only let Mum pack rice and curry into our school lunch boxes that first time! After that it was devon and tomato sauce or ham and yellow pickle sandwiches, or better still, some money so that we could buy a meat pie.

We came to the Tamar Valley in 1988 from the madness of Sydney, our own bicentennial project, on our way to Hobart to start a new life. Somehow, we never made it and have spent the last 25 years very happily living in this amazing region. During the course of these 25 years I have discovered for myself, the amazing light, and subtle nuances of the landscape. The Tamar Valley has been a happy hunting ground for me when I set off to make pictures, and being able to include my favourite images of the Valley has been one of the delights of working on this book.

My work as a photographer brought me in contact with John and Danielle almost at the very start of my time here, so it has been great to be able to work with them on this project. It is always good to work with people who are passionate about what they do, and these two are no exception.

Our aim was to really shine a spotlight on the wonderful food that this area has to offer and the dedicated people who produce it. Along the way I was amazed, enthralled and educated by the people who have dedicated their lives to producing the best food that they can. That singularity of purpose has always been very appealing to me, regardless of what people are trying to achieve. When you mix this beautiful, hand grown produce with the talent and passion that John brings from so many years of thinking only about food and how to cook it, the results are astounding.

During the course of this project, I have tried just about every dish in the book. I have also been learning how to cook, with the tips and tricks from a master chef, given so readily. It has been an absolute pleasure working with John, we have always got on well and our interests of food, fishing and rugby makes it an easy partnership.

My thanks, as always go to my wife, and partner in everything, Vicki who has managed the whole project, designed the book and basically made it happen. This is not an unusual situation for us - I tend to have a never ending series of ideas, and it is usually Vicki who makes them happen. This is a system that we have used and prospered by for the last 30 years, so I am not about to over analyse it or try and change it.

I would also like to thank John's wife Lee, who has put up with us turning her home into a commercial kitchen/photographic studio for weeks at a time, who has spent many a night typing recipes and turning John's notes and writings into something that we can all read!

Ian Wallace, has held my hand every time I get it into my head to do a book, he makes sure that it is all ready for the printer and that it comes back to us looking exactly the way we expected it to look. Thanks Ian, you have taught us how to do this, but I would never think of doing a book without you!

Finally I would like to say thank you to Richard Bennett who inspired me to start this project and who has always been the perfect combination of mentor and great mate.

Philip Kuruvita

tamar valley pantry

many thanks to...

First and foremost to Philip Kuruvita, for the invitation to do something I have been waiting to achieve for a long time. I am truly grateful in his belief that we could achieve our goal. Oh, and his great photography might be worth a mention!!

To his wife, Vicki - behind every good man there is an even better woman to drive them. Vicki has spent literally hours compiling information, photos and recipes then publishing to create what I believe to be a real winner in the "Tamar Valley Pantry".

To all the producers who trusted our concept in the beginning and in particular Tasmanian Hotel & Catering Supplies who provided the majority of the props for the photo shoots.

To my mother who is a great cook. She always provided warm hearty meals that I cherish from my childhood, in particular the baking smells coming from the AGA or café kitchen at the Knowe Guest House in Port Patrick, Scotland.

My father, who gave me the freedom to choose my own career. Although a lover of well cooked meat, he too enjoyed some of the finer things in life – aged meats, oysters, black pudding, potted shrimps, roast duck and of course, cheeses. Tasty Lancashire that bit your head off was his favourite!

Mr Anton Mosimann of Mosimann's Belgrave London. During the late 70's and through the 80's his kitchens at the Dorchester Hotel, London were the starting point for many chefs' culinary journeys. The sheer size of the place - 120 strong chef brigade was overwhelming. Most of his chefs are now the world's leading chefs. His belief and philosophy on food and how it was prepared and presented was way ahead of its time and an inspiration to many. His passion to promote young chefs, bringing them out from behind the walls and giving them the recognition they deserved was the beginning of the television chefs we see today.

Danielle Blewitt, not only for her honest words but for 20 years of friendship and for writing so passionately about food and the great State of Tasmania, in particular the Tamar Valley. This just happens to be where Danielle, Philip and I all hit Tassie at the same time late in 1989.

To my wife Lee for her unconditional love, support and bloody hard graft - you have always given 110% in everything. We are still here together so let's take this to another chapter - all my love John.

Last but certainly not least, Andrew "Bear" Christie. For those of you who haven't yet been touched by him, an inspirational, exciting, and knowledgeable man, so generous with his culinary knowledge with a wonderful, infectious personality - Thank you for 30 years of friendship, love and laughter.

John T. Bailey

15

suppliers

21	bilambil berry farm
26	bridestowe lavender estate
32	cocobean chocolate
41	coronea grove olives
46	four springs produce
55	goaty hill wines
60	harvest farmers' market
66	hillwood farmgate
75	honey tasmania
83	josef chromy wines
90	landfall farm fresh
98	leaning church vineyard
107	lees orchard
114	lilydale larder
122	manubread
128	nigel's gourmet on tamar
140	ritual coffee
150	rosevears waterfront tavern
156	tamar valley truffles
164	tasmanian hotel and catering supplies
172	the mill providore and gallery
180	trevallyn grocer
186	van dieman brewing
195	vélo wines
202	westhaven dairy
210	wild fish
217	ye olde green grocer

tamar valley pantry

recipes

22	blueberry clafoutis
24	blueberry + pink grapefruit sorbet
28	lavender chicken
30	lavender + honey icecream
34	chocolate torte
36	chocolate genoese sponge
36	orange + star anise sauce
38	white chocolate brownie
42	salmon + fennel carpaccio
44	blue eye cod romesco
48	tomato + fennel tart
50	roasted purple garlic aioli
56	bbq quail
58	mussel broth
62	duck confit
64	thai beef salad
68	strawberry millefeuille
70	strawberry flambe
76	prickly box honey panna cotta
76	rhubarb compote
78	honey + pistachio fudge
78	crystallized pistachios
84	three cheese fondue
86	rabbit cassoulet
92	oyster blade steak tagliata
94	pulled lamb noisette

100	chicken + pistachio terrine
102	warm strawberry salad
108	pink lady apple custard tart
110	warm pear en croute
116	free range egg omelette
118	chèvre tart
124	hot smoked ocean trout on rye
126	sweet fruit brioche pudding
130	hot smoked salmon risotto
132	chorizo sausage linguine
136	chick pea + vegetable curry
138	seared tuna tataki
142	coffee parfait
144	coffee crème brulée
146	coffee shortbread
146	coffee granita
152	tasmanian wallaby fillets
154	char grilled veal rib eye
158	potted duck + truffle jelly
160	truffle consommé en surprise
166	crispy pork belly
168	lamb primal rump roast
174	seared wild harc's loin
176	sloe gin cheesecake
176	chocolate + orange fudge
182	tasmanian scallops
184	boerewors sausage
188	slow cooked pork hock
190	short cut beef ribs
196	roasted venison medallions
198	pizza de fruits de mere
204	palak paneer
206	roasted beetroot + chèvre salad
212	poached blue eye cod
214	smoked fish kedgeree
218	smoky mushroom mélange
220	pumpkin + baby spinach salad
224	chicken and beef stock
225	chicken stock
225	fish stock
226	marinated vegetable stock
226	basil pesto
226	balsamic syrup
227	chilli oil
227	herb oil
227	garlic oil
228	crème patisserie
228	tuile biscuits
228	shortcrust pastry

bilambil berry farm

Bilambil Berry Farm is a family run, boutique blueberry farm on 10 hectares at Turners Marsh.

Established almost 30 years ago, the orchard contains about 2000 blueberry plants. Fifteen years ago the farm adopted organic management practices and within three years received organic certification from Tasmanian Organic-Dynamic Producers.

Kent and Alyssa Mainwaring took over the property four years ago. They have embarked on an extensive program to upgrade the orchard and the farm infrastructure, including replacing under performing plants, upgrading the packing shed and other out buildings, renovations to the family home and general farm beautification works. Kent and Alyssa have embraced the principles of organic production and their goal is to produce the very best blueberries without the use of any chemical inputs. The last harvest produced more than eight tonnes of premium fruit – the majority of which was sent to wholesalers in Sydney, Melbourne and Adelaide.

The only local outlet they supply is Ye Olde Green Grocer in Launceston. During the harvest, which lasts for about seven weeks, Kent's eldest son Fraser assumes the position of Orchard Manager. The youngest member of the family, Will, helps out in the packing shed. Kent and Alyssa have a focus on employing people from the local area. Many of their staff members have worked on the property every season for 10 years or more.

Kent and Alyssa are very positive about the future. They are confident that demand for their premium product will remain strong and that they can increase fruit yield. They believe they are proof that from even a relatively small land holding it is possible to create a financially viable enterprise founded on sustainable principles.

tamar valley pantry
bilambil organic blueberries

blueberry clafoutis

serves 8

ingredients

85g flaked almonds, toasted
25g plain flour
pinch of sea salt
140g caster sugar
3 large free range eggs
4 large free range yolks
375mls double cream

375g Bilambil organic blueberries
butter to grease dishes
icing sugar sifted

NB: fresh or frozen berries can be used in this recipe

method

Grind the almonds in a food processor till fine.
Blend flour and salt.
Add the sugar, whole eggs, yolks and cream.
Blend until batter is creamy smooth.
(You can store this in a jug in the fridge for up to 24 hours should you wish)
Pre heat the oven to 180°C.
Butter eight 10cm gratin dishes.
Scatter blueberries over the bottom.
Give the batter a stir and pour into dishes.
Bake for 18-20 minutes until risen and slightly firm.
Dust with icing sugar.

"Serve warm with your favourite ice cream, double cream or as shown, with a vanilla crème anglaise"

tamar valley pantry
bilambil organic blueberries

blueberry + pink grapefruit sorbet

ingredients

serves 6

350g organic blueberries frozen preferred
125g peeled and diced pink grapefruit
150g caster sugar
300g cubed ice
2 egg whites

1 lemon juiced

Keep a few blueberries and grapefruit segments aside for a salad

method

Blend blueberries and caster sugar in a Thermomix™ (a very smart blender!).
Add the grapefruit flesh and lemon juice, then add the ice 1/3 at a time, blending each time.
Once all the ice has been added, add the egg whites and blend for a further 2 minutes..
Place in the freezer for at least 4 - 6 hours before serving.
Serve with the mixed fruits and your favourite tuile biscuit (recipe pg 228).

"For this recipe I have used a Thermomix™. What an amazing machine! it has become my little apprentice without the backchat !"

bridestowe lavender estate

Established in 1922, Bridestowe Estate is an acclaimed supplier of the finest lavender oils for the world fragrance market. The vast fields of luscious lavender blooms have become an iconic tourist destination in North East Tasmania. Each year, more than 55,000 visitors travel to the site to experience the sensory delights of the plantations and the stunning landscapes.

Whilst Bridestowe Estate has always been a world leader in the production of fine lavender oil, it was only in the 1950's that a selective breeding program successfully unlocked the secrets of the unique fragrance. Today, the oils from five individual clones of *Lavandula angustifolia* are distilled and blended to produce the world-renowned Bridestowe Lavender Oil. At the same time, an integrated harvesting and distilling procedure was pioneered using equipment designed on the site. This streamlined the harvesting and distillation and further improved the quality and longevity of the oil.

Under new ownership, Bridestowe Estate again embarked on an innovative, award-winning research and development program. Emphasis was directed to the culinary potential of lavender. Whilst lavender has long been regarded as one of the most traditional flavouring herbs, it was the selection of "Bridestowe Philippa" for culinary lavender purposes that lead to the development of the Bridestowe GOURMET range. The careful drying and stabilising techniques at Bridestowe Estate capture and preserve the sweet floral aromas for use for use in a wide variety of applications.

Now, fine fruit flavours and spices can be harmoniously intertwined with Bridestowe GOURMET Culinary Lavender to produce extraordinary results. A recipe development program has optimised guidelines for the use of lavender in cooking.

The Bridestowe Lavender Estate is beautiful throughout the seasons, with peak flowering in late Spring and Summer.

tamar valley pantry
bridestowe gourmet culinary lavender

lavender chicken
with french mustard and lavender

serves 6

ingredients

1 kg chicken thighs or breast fillets
olive oil
butter
4-6 small-medium onions cut into quarters
125g smoky bacon or pancetta, diced
1 cup dry Tamar Valley white wine (we used Semillon)
2 cups chicken stock
2 tbsp dijon mustard
3 tsp Bridestowe GOURMET Culinary Lavender
½ cup cream
salt and pepper
2 tbsp chopped parsley

method

Heat oil and butter, add onions.
Cook until the onions soften slightly. Remove and set aside.
Brown chicken and bacon.
Pour in stock and wine and add mustard, lavender, salt and pepper.
Return onions to pan.
Bring to boil and cook for 30-45 minutes until chicken is just tender.
Strain off sauce into another saucepan.
Add the cream and reduce to desired consistency.
Pour thickened sauce over chicken, reheat.
Sprinkle with parsley and serve with potatoes and crusty bread.

"Wonderful accompanied with a Tamar Valley Chardonnay"

recipe supplied by bridestowe lavender estate

tamar valley pantry

bridestowe gourmet lavender flower honey

lavender + honey icecream

ingredients

serves 6

2 tsp Bridestowe GOURMET Culinary Lavender
1 cup milk
1 cup cream
180g caster sugar

2 tbsp Bridestowe GOURMET Lavender Flower Honey
5 egg yolks
1 tsp vanilla extract

method

Grind the Bridestowe GOURMET Culinary Lavender in a spice or coffee grinder with 1 tablespoon of the sugar. Put the milk and cream into a saucepan and add the sugar, the ground lavender and the Bridestowe GOURMET Lavender Flower Honey to the milk and cream and bring the mixture to boiling point. Allow to cool slightly.

Beat the egg yolks until light and foamy. Pour the milk and cream mixture over the egg yolks and stir until well mixed. Return to the saucepan which has been rinsed out and cook over a moderate heat stirring constantly until the mixture thickens and coats the back of a spoon. Add vanilla. Cover with plastic wrap and cool.

Strain the custard mixture and churn in an icecream maker according to the manufacturer's instructions.

"This luscious icecream takes a little time to make but the results are well worth the effort!"

recipe supplied by bridestowe lavender estate

tamar valley pantry

cocobean chocolate

It may be a petite, hole-in-the-wall style shop, but Cocobean Chocolate in Launceston has a big, burly reputation as the city's own chocolate institution.

Locals and visitors alike get their chocolate fix from behind the counter of this boutique establishment located in the heart – or perhaps that should be stomach – of Launceston's CBD!

Chocolatier Theresa Streefland's vision is that people experience the decadent stuff on more than one level: Taste, aroma, texture, presentation and education.

"Chocolate is more than confectionary," she insists.

Cocobean uses only the finest ingredients, including couverture from Swiss company Felchlin, which has an outstanding reputation for supporting all people involved in the chain of cocoa production. Whatever the choice from Cocobean's menu – hot chocolate, handmade truffles, chocolate mousse, chocolate taste plate, chocolate milkshake, chocolate ice-cream – the selection is guilt-free.

Cocobean is very much a family business, founded in 2008 by husband and wife team Rick and Theresa Streefland, who have involved their three adult children in its operation in

some capacity over its history, whether serving in the café, making chocolates or crunching numbers.

Demand for the Cocobean product expanded so much that the on-site kitchen was outgrown in 2011. Chocolate is now manufactured at a larger, purpose-built kitchen in Kings Meadows. Cocobean is also distributed via the wholesale market and the continued success of this quality Tasmanian brand means you are likely to see Cocobean Chocolate boutiques popping up around the state.

tamar valley pantry
cocobean dark coverture chocolate

chocolate torte
with orange, star anise and pinot noir sauce

makes
1 large
or 2 small
tortes

ingredients

chocolate mousse
300g dark coverture chocolate
80g butter, chopped
2tbsp cocoa powder, sifted
5 sheets leaf gelatine, pre-soaked in water

4 eggs, separated
500ml thickened cream
3tbsp icing sugar
cocoa powder for dusting

method

Place chocolate, cocoa powder & butter in a saucepan on a low heat until melted and smooth.
Remove from heat, add gelatine and mix through until dissolved.
In a separate bowl, pour mixture over egg yolks; beat & put aside.
Whisk cream to soft peaks and set aside.
Place egg whites in a mixer and whisk, gradually adding icing sugar.
Take 1/3 of egg whites mixture and beat into the chocolate mixture, then fold in the rest of the mixture.
Add cream and fold into the mixture.
Pour onto sponge (recipe pg 36) and set for 2-3 hours in the refrigerator.
Dust with cocoa powder.
Remove from the torte rings by gently using a blow torch to remove the frame, then remove paper.
Cut and serve with orange, star anise and pinot noir sauce (recipe pg 36).

chocolate genoese sponge
for chocolate torte

makes 1 large or 2 small tortes

ingredients

5 free range eggs, whole
150g caster sugar
30g butter, melted
115g plain flour
40g cocoa powder

method

Pre heat oven 180°C.
Sift flour and cocoa powder together and set aside.
In a bowl, over warm water, place eggs, sugar and butter and whisk until very pale (5-6 minutes).
Remove from heat and whisk until cool. You should have a trail left behind on the whisk.
Add the cocoa and flour mixture - 1/3 first, then fold the rest through.
Pour into cake tin and bake for 12-15 minutes until just firm.
Remove from oven. Cool before tipping onto cooling wire.
Once cool, cut discs out to fit inside torte rings lined with baking paper.

orange + star anise sauce
with pinot noir

ingredients

4 oranges, peeled and segmented, keep skins
1 cinnamon stick
1 bay leaf
1 star anise
115g caster sugar
200ml pinot noir

method

Place orange segments and skins in a saucepan with all other ingredients. Bring to boil.
Reduce over slower heat until syrupy consistency. Strain. Cool & serve.

"You may wish to use mandarins in season - if so use 6 mandarins"

37

tamar valley pantry
cocobean white chocolate raspberries

white chocolate brownie
with chilli and raspberries

serves 6

ingredients

200g butter
300g white chocolate
3 whole free range eggs
½tsp vanilla essence
150g plain flour sifted
pinch of salt
10g freeze dried raspberries pieces
2g freeze dried raspberry powder, sifted for garnish
12 Cocobean White Chocolate Raspberries for garnish

chillies

1 large red chilli, seeds removed
1 large green chilli, seeds removed
100g caster sugar
150mls water

method

Pre- heat the oven to 180°C.
Spray and line a 20cm x 30cm baking tray.
Finely slice chillies on an angle, Chinese style into a pot.
Combine sugar, water, chillies and simmer for 5 minutes.
Allow to cool.
in a large bowl, over a water bath, melt ½ the chocolate and butter, then remove from heat source.
In a separate, bowl beat the eggs, sugar and vanilla until very pale, then beat through the chocolate mixture.
Fold in the flour and salt, then the remaining white chocolate chopped into pieces.
Drain the chillies and add with the raspberry pieces to the batter.
Pour into baking pan and bake till golden and soft to touch - approximately 25 minutes. Remove and cool in the pan.
Cut into large squares, dust with the raspberry powder.
Add a chocolate raspberry to each piece and serve on a large platter garnished with fresh chillies.

"You can add more chillies if you wish - depending on your palate"

39

coronea grove olives

Coronea Grove Olives is a family owned and operated olive grove located close to Launceston that produces one of the finest olive oils available.

It consists of 750 trees, the first of which were planted in 2000. A number of varieties were initially trialled but those that proved most successful in the cold and sometimes frosty environment are Frantoio and Leccino, both traditional Tuscan varieties.

The premium oil is from the Frantoio variety. Beautifully green and peppery, it is well balanced with both some bitterness and pungency producing a complex fruity Extra Virgin Olive Oil. The Leccino variety provides a smooth buttery oil with some peppery after tastes that is ideal for all purpose everyday uses. It is also a deep green colour that looks fantastic on the plate when poured from its one litre cask.

A desire to benchmark the Coronea Grove olive oil against the best in Australia means that it is regularly entered in the Australian Olive Association National Olive Oil Show. Since the first Gold Medal and Best in Class in 2007, Coronea Grove has been consistent medal winners of gold, silver and bronze awards.

They are committed to best practice in all areas of production from careful tree planting and pruning through to immediate post-harvest cold pressing. They are also a signatory to the Australian Olive Industry Code of Practice, which certifies the authenticity and freshness of the olive oil, with a distinctive logo attached to their oil containers.

"At Coronea Grove, our production will never be huge but we will continue to concentrate on producing well balanced, cool climate Extra Virgin Olive Oil - the perfect oil for you to enjoy every day!"

tamar valley pantry
coronea grove olive oil

salmon + fennel carpaccio

ingredients

serves 4

300g sashimi grade salmon, skinned and boned
1 small fennel bulb
2 lemons, juiced
1½ tsp sugar
80ml Coronea Grove Olive Oil

1tsp mint, chopped finely
1tbsp dill, chopped
40g baby capers
sea salt
cracked pepper

method

Wash the fennel bulb, then slice paper thin using a mandolin slicer.
Place the lemon juice in a bowl with the sugar and dissolve.
Slice the salmon sashimi style and lay out on serving platter. You may wish to part freeze the salmon wrapped in plastic to make slicing easier.
Add the herbs to the lemon juice and whisk through the olive oil before adding the fennel and baby capers.
Season lightly, spoon over the raw fish evenly and serve.

"the lemon juice will start to cook the salmon so add it just before serving "

blue eye cod romesco
with breadcrumb and almond crust

serves 4

ingredients

breadcrumbs
1 tsp garlic granules
1 tbsp. paprika
1 tbsp. smoked paprika
50g toasted flaked almonds
50g fine white breadcrumbs

fish
4 x 180g blue eye cod fillets, deboned
4 tbsp Coronea Grove Olive Oil
sea salt

emulsion
200ml milk, full cream
1 garlic clove
180ml olive oil
50g almonds, whole blanched

chives for garnish optional

method

breadcrumbs
Put all the ingredients into a food processor and blitz til you have a very fine breadcrumb texture. Set aside.

fish
Vacuum seal each piece of blue eye cod with a little salt and 1 tbsp. of olive oil. Cook in a bain marie or sous-vide bath for 12 minutes at 60°C

emulsion
In a saucepan, boil the milk with the almonds and the garlic. Blend with stick blender, drizzling in the oil until the sauce thickens.
Add the liquid from the fish bags until you have the desired consistency.

Pat the fish dry with paper towel before coating with the breadcrumbs mix on the top.
Pour a pool of sauce on to a warm bowl and place fish. Drizzle with a few drops of olive oil.
Garnish with long chives and 2 or 3 flaked toasted almonds.

"Many types of fish would be suitable for this dish but I would certainly recommend fillets only"

45

tamar valley pantry

four springs produce

Annette and Nevil Reed know just what their consumers mean when they say, "I want a tomato that tastes like a tomato and I want garlic with real flavour"!

It was on their Selbourne property, just half an hour's drive from Launceston, that the Reeds fell in love with heirloom tomatoes.

"We started growing 40 heirloom varieties for a Tasmanian seed distributor, to complement our garlic, truffle and Dorper lamb production. We'd never grown a tomato from seed before and in our first year grew 1600. From that very first crop we were hooked," Annette said.

While the Reeds still produce tomato seed, their passion is for the colour, taste and variety that are found in fresh, field-grown, chemical-free produce.

Throughout the Summer tomato season, you will find Four Springs Produce heirloom tomatoes at the Launceston Harvest Farmer's Market and at selected local restaurants.

"We find great satisfaction in being able to meet our customer's specific needs and to teach the uninitiated about our products. A tomato is not just a tomato! The slower growing and vine ripening process of our heirloom tomatoes produces more distinctive, individual flavours. Red, yellow, green, black or orange; early, mid and late fruiting; rich and tangy or sweet and mild, there is a special tomato to meet every taste and requirement." Nevil added.

Along with tomatoes, the Reeds produce an exceptionally well-flavoured Purple Stripe Garlic. Planted by hand into rich, red Selbourne soil, every clove develops into a rich, flavoursome bulb. None of the garlic is wasted, with many of the earlier scapes being processed into a delicious mild salt prior to the main harvest. The fresh garlic is mainly sold locally and is also available as quality seed.

tamar valley pantry
four springs tomatoes

tomato + fennel tart
with basil mascarpone

serves 4-6

ingredients

2 baby fennel bulbs, sliced fine
2 golden shallots, sliced fine
2 gloves garlic, sliced fine
olive oil
75g dark brown sugar
200ml white balsamic vinegar or
    sherry vinegar
2 bay leaves
2 sprigs of thyme
100g basil pesto (recipe pg 226)
60g mascarpone
400g Four Springs Tommy Toe
    Tomatoes, halved
4-6 short crust pastry tart shells
    (recipe pg 228)
10-12 pieces shaved pecorino
chilli oil (recipe pg 227)
balsamic syrup (recipe pg 226)

method

In a heavy based saucepan heat a little oil and fry the fennel, shallots and garlic until golden and caramelized.
Add the brown sugar, vinegar, bay leaves and thyme.
Reduce the mixture on high heat, stirring all the time for 10-15 minutes.
Cool the fennel jam down and reserve for later.
Mix the mascarpone and pesto - it will thicken slightly.
Place a dessert spoon of the fennel jam in the base of each tart shell.
In a non-stick frying pan, heat a little oil.
Add the tomato halves and flash fry, cut side down first, until they acheive a rich caramel appearance.
Place the tomatoes evenly on the jam.
Top with a quenelle of pesto and mascarpone mix.
Garnish with shaved pecorino and present with chilli oil and balsamic syrup just before serving.

"The secret to this dish is the full flavoured tomatoes and fresh ingredients."

tamar valley pantry
four springs purple garlic

roasted purple stripe garlic aioli
with hand cut chips triple cooked

serves 6

ingredients

1kg potatoes, peeled and cut into 2 x 2 x 6cm chips
groundnut oil or grape seed oil
sea salt flakes
2 heads of purple stripe garlic
a little oil

aioli
3 large free range egg yolks
30g dijon mustard
1½ head of garlic
350g of ½ olive and ½ nut oil
35g white wine vinegar
½ tsp sea salt
pinch ground white pepper

method

Place the hand cut chips in a bowl of running water and rinse off the starch.
Simmer chips in a pot of water for 20 minutes until just soft. Remove carefully and drain on cooling rack.
Place the chips in the freezer for at least 1 hour to remove moisture.
Heat the grape seed oil in a deep fryer to 130°C.
Fry the chips in small batches til a light crust is formed. Drain on kitchen paper.
Cool again in the freezer.
Turn the oil up to 180°C. Fry the chips till golden and crunchy - approximately 7 minutes. Drain and sprinkle with sea salt flakes and serve.

aioli
Roast garlic in oven at 180°C for 20 minutes. Set aside and once cooled, pop cloves from one head of garlic into a bowl. Retain the rest of the garlic for serving. Add the egg yolks and mustard, blend with a stick blender. Drizzle the oil into the mixture very slowly while blending to create an emulsification.
As the mixture thickens, add the vinegar to thin down and continue to add the rest of the oil.
Finally, season and serve with the remainder of the garlic intact for presentation.

"Egg yolks are amazing - 1 single egg yolk can hold up to 2 litres of oil"

windermere church on the tamar

goaty hill wines

Knowing the seasonal workings of their vineyard and making and tasting the fruits of that labour, are all part of the journey undertaken by two families to discover the educated enjoyment of fine wine.

Goaty Hill Wines is a leading boutique family owned and operated vineyard at Kayena in Tasmania's Tamar Valley. The Goaty Hill family takes great pride in their 20-hectare vineyard and believes excellence in winemaking starts with the vines.

While Goaty Hill Wines will celebrate its eighth commercial vintage in 2013, the actual vineyard in the picturesque West Tamar Region of Tasmania is now 15 years old. In 1998 partners in the venture moved from Victoria to Tasmania to follow their dream of starting a vineyard and ultimately a wine label. They had decided to live their life doing something that offered a challenge in an industry and location they felt passionate about.

It was in 2005, the Goaty Hill Wines partners decided to launch a wine label that encapsulated their passion for quality and enjoyment of fine Tasmanian wine.

Together with their winemaker, they followed their philosophy of allowing the vineyard characteristics to show through into the wines. This minimalist approach to the winemaking process has produced some outstanding indicative cool climate wines with a list of trophies, awards and gold medals flowing from their first vintage.

In considering a name for their label, partners turned to their vineyard for inspiration. A notable landmark on the property is a steep and rocky hill offering panoramic views of the region, locally-known as Goaty Hill.

tamar valley pantry
goaty hill pinot noir

bbq quail
on grilled polenta with rhubarb, fresh thyme + pinot reduction

serves 6

ingredients

6 de-boned Rannoch farm quail, marinated in garlic + fresh thyme oil
250ml of chicken and beef stock (recipe pg 224)
150ml Goaty Hill Pinot Noir
1 golden shallot, peeled and finely chopped
a little oil

400 rhubarb, cut into 7.5cm pieces
2 tbsp sugar
1 orange, juice and zest

125g of polenta, fine
250ml hot chicken stock (recipe pg 225)
25g butter
2 tsp chopped thyme
salt + pepper
olive oil
sprig of thyme for garnish

method

Place the polenta, butter, stock, thyme and seasoning in a pot and bring to the boil.
Reduce heat and cook through for 3-4 minutes until smooth and not grainy - stirring all the time.
Lightly oil a small roasting pan and pour polenta in.
Place in the fridge to set for at least 1 hour.
Cut squares and bar mark on chargrill.
Keep warm until you serve.

Place the washed, peeled and cut rhubarb in a baking tray. Sprinkle with the orange zest, juice and sugar then bake at 200°C for 10-15 minutes until just softened. Allow to cool.

Preheat the BBQ. Cook quail, skin side first, to give a crisscross barmark effect.

Sauté the shallots in a little oil to brown slightly.
Add the wine and reduce by half. Add the stock and again reduce by half so you have a syrup like consistency.
Cut the quail in half, length ways. Place on top of the warm polenta. Spread the pieces of rhubarb around the plate then pour the sauce around.
Garnish with fresh thyme sprig.

"Rannoch farm produces the very best quail in Tasmania if not Australia and combines perfectly with the luscious cherry and plum fruits and soft tannins of this wonderful Tasmanian Pinot Noir"

tamar valley pantry
goaty hill riesling

mussel broth
with garden fresh herbs

ingredients

serves 4

1kg wild Tasmanian mussels
2 kaffir lime leaves, torn
1 shallot, finely diced
2 gloves garlic, finely chopped
75ml Goaty Hill Riesling
150ml fish stock (recipe pg 225)
1 tsp fresh flat leaf parsley
1 tsp fresh tarragon or dill

method

Clean and de-beard the mussels.
Heat a drizzle of oil in a heavy large pot. Add the garlic and shallot, but do not brown.
Add the white wine, fish stock and kaffir lime leaves and bring to a fast boil.
Add the mussels and most of the chopped herbs, placing a lid over them.
Pour into warm serving bowls and sprinkle with the rest of the herbs. Serve with warm crusty bread.

"There is a bit of a myth about fresh mussels - if they don't open - discard them. I dispute that. I have had mussels so fresh and so tight the sphincter mussel has not released during cooking.

I say if the mussels in the shell don't weigh heavy then there is a problem."

tamar valley pantry

harvest farmers' market

Harvest Launceston Community Farmers' Market brightens a quiet inner city car park every Saturday morning when up to 50 seasonal producers bring their produce to Launceston from all corners of Tasmania.

Here, you can find a wonderful variety of Tasmanian produce including fruit, vegetables, meat, dairy, seasonal preserves, artisan bread, oils, beer, wine and cider.

Harvest Launceston is an authentic weekly farmers' market bringing the world's best produce from the producer to the people. The market adheres to a strict charter and the Australian Farmers' Market Association guidelines.

As a not-for-profit organisation, Harvest is a true community market where locals are involved in running and setting up the market every weekend.

Launched in February 2012, Harvest Launceston is a vibrant social and shopping event, attracting people to the centre of town to meet and talk to those who grow, catch, bake, make, brew or produce their food.

Seasonal produce is celebrated every weekend and there's plenty to feast on site from gourmet grilled cheese sandwiches and vegan laksa to Turkish gozleme and locally roasted coffee.

Harvest Launceston Community Farmers' Market is held every Saturday from 8.30am – 12.30pm in the Cimitiere Street car park (opposite Albert Hall).

duck confit
roasted root vegetables, golden shallot + pinot noir reduction

serves 6

ingredients

6 duck maryland

duck rub
2 tbsp sea salt
3 gloves of garlic, peeled whole
1 tbsp cracked pepper
1 tsp chopped fresh thyme

500ml duck fat, melted
1 whole turnip, peeled
2 whole carrots, peeled
1 whole swede, peeled
3 golden shallots
1 golden shallot, finely chopped
olive oil
150ml pinot noir
500ml chicken stock, reduce with high heat to 250ml thick jus
1 tsp parsley, thyme and sage, chopped

method

The day before: Rub the duck legs with the seasoning and cryovac. Leave overnight in the fridge.

Remove the duck legs from the cryovac pouch and gently rinse the salt off.

Place in another cryovac bag and add the just melted duck fat then seal the bag.

Place in a sous-vide bath for 12 hours at 70°C

Part steam the root vegetables including the whole shallots. Fry in a little duck fat first, then bake in a hot oven at 200°C.

Sauté the chopped shallot in a little oil before adding the wine. Reduce by ½ the volume then add the jus and reduce by half again. Keep warm.

Remove the duck legs and carefully place on a wire rack or a baking tray and roast to colour in the oven.

Arrange the vegetables on a warm plate, add the chopped herbs. Pour the sauce around the plate and place the duck leg on top and serve.

"I have chosen to use the cookery method sous-vide that allows moist delicate cooking to retain all the integrity of the product without shrinking"

thai beef salad
with fried shallots

serves 4

ingredients

300g beef sirloin steak, seasoned, cooked rare to medium - well rested but still warm then sliced into thin strips for serving
¼ chinese wonbok cabbage
2 fresh tomatoes, sliced & de-seeded
1 piece of cucumber, de-seeded, sliced thinly
½ red onion, sliced finely
3 spring onions, sliced on a 45° angle

a small handful thai basil leaves, chopped at the last minute

a handful of coriander leaves and stem, also chopped last minute
1 tbsp fried shallots - from asian stores
2 tsp toasted sesame seeds
1 fresh lime for garnish, cut in cheeks

dressing

2 tbsp palm sugar liquid
2 limes, juiced
90ml fish sauce
40ml oyster sauce
2 red chilies birds eye, chopped very finely

method

dressing: Place the chillies in a bowl and whisk together with the oyster sauce, fish sauce and fresh lime juice. Add palm sugar to taste. Set aside.

Finely slice the wonbok leaves. Place in a large mixing bowl and add the rest of the salad ingredients - tomatoes, cucumber, red onion, spring onions.
Add the beef to the salad, then add the dressing - save the dressing until the last minute to avoid soggy salad. Now quickly add the herbs and arrange on a serving plate.
Sprinkle with toasted sesame seeds and fried shallots. Garnish with cheeks of fresh lime

"Thai flavours for this dish are hot, salty & sweet !
You may also wish to add noodles to this but you will need
more dressing to maintain the flavour"

hillwood farmgate

Hilllwood Farmgate evolved from the diversification of Robin Dornauf's dairy business Meander Valley Dairy. Robin started Meander Valley Dairy in 2003 using his life experience and knowledge of dairy farming to produce some of Australia's finest double cream, crème fraiche, clotted cream, cultured butter and ice cream.

In 2010, having outgrown their existing factory in Launceston, Robin and his sons, Simon and Marcus, moved the business out to Hillwood. While their dairy business is still called Meander Valley Dairy (despite being in the Tamar Valley) the farm where everything is produced is now called Hillwood Farmgate.

On 100 acres overlooking the Tamar River, there was enough space for the factory plus some other projects, so Robin and his son Simon took the opportunity to grow strawberries. Growing their crop in purpose-built poly tunnels, they produce some of the finest fruit on the market.

Hillwood Farmgate uses the philosophy of supplying "single touch fruit" to the market. Their strawberries are field picked daily wth minimal handling of the fruit. The fruit is weighed, labelled and packed ready for market within minutes of coming off the plant and is sold Australia wide.

Never ones to rest on their laurels, the Dornaufs have many future plans for the farm. High up on the list is to expand the berry business with work well underway towards introducing other varieties such as raspberries and blackberries into the mix.

Currently their shop is open over the strawberry season from November to June and people can purchase fresh produce direct from the Farmgate. Their vision is to have a farm shop and restaurant where people can taste, buy and enjoy their products whilst learning about their food's journey from paddock to plate.

tamar valley pantry
hillwood farmgate driscoll strawberries

strawberry millefeuille

serves 6

ingredients

500g Hillwood Farmgate Driscoll Strawberries
350g good puff pastry (eg:carême all butter puff)
1 quantity crème patisserie (recipe pg 228)
350g extra strawberries
150g caster sugar

150ml water
Icing sugar
extra caster sugar for rolling

method

Pre heat the oven to 200°C

On a lightly floured surface, add a little caster sugar and roll out the pastry to a rectangle 28 x 30cm.

Place on a baking tray lined with baking paper. Place another baking paper sheet on top and weigh down with a ceramic oven dish and bake for 25-30 minutes until pastry is golden and crisp. Set aside to cool.

When completely cooled, trim the edges and cut into 2 or 3 rectangles, making sure they are equal sizes.

Heat the extra strawberries in the sugar and water, then cook for 5 minutes.

Pass through a fine sieve, then chill the coulis completely.

To assemble, lay a rectangle piece of pastry on a serving tray. Pipe the crème patisserie on the base. Place the cut strawberries on top.

Pipe further crème patisserie on top before placing the top piece of pastry, then cut with a serrated knife to portion.

Place a pool of strawberry coulis on the serving plate and carefully place your millefeuille in the centre. Dust heavily with sifted icing sugar and serve.

"The coulis retains a beautiful strawberry colour if passed through a fine sieve rather than blended with a bamix or processor "

tamar valley pantry
hillwood farmgate strawberries

strawberry flambe
with honeycomb mascarpone and cointreau

ingredients

serves 4

400g Hillwood Farmgate Strawberries, hulled and cut in ½
100ml dessert wine or sparkling wine
1tbsp icing sugar
200g mascarpone
125ml ready to serve custard
1 vanilla bean, split and seeds scrapped out

butter
25ml cointreau
biscotti biscuits

honeycomb (can be substituted with 2 crunchie bars)
75g caster sugar
2 tbsp golden syrup
2 tsp bicarbonate of soda, sifted

method

Place the strawberries, icing sugar and dessert wine in a bowl. Cover and allow to macerate for about ½ hour

For the honeycomb, grease a baking tray with butter and set aside.
In a deep pan, warm the sugar and golden syrup over low heat til dissolved, then increase the heat to medium without stirring for 5- 10 minutes or until thickened and changed colour to a dark golden caramel. Remove the pan from the heat and add the bicarb of soda. Be careful as the reaction will foam rapidly. Pour into baking tray and cool. Once cooled, break the honeycomb into chunks.

In a bowl, mix the mascarpone, custard and vanilla seeds together.
Drain strawberries and reserve syrup. Flame the cointreau in a large frying pan and add the strawberries for 1-2 minutes. Remove and chill slightly.
To serve, place broken biscotti biscuits in the bottom of the glass. Layer the mascarpone, honeycomb (or crunchie bars) and strawberries in the glass.
Finish by pouring the strawberry wine syrup over the dish then serve.

"Toffee and caramel can burn you severely. Yes speaking from experience!! so have a bowl of ice water on standby whenever dealing with hot toffee!"

batman bridge on the tamar

74

honey tasmania

It took only a few years of living in the beautiful Tamar Valley for the Campbell family to realise that the area was ideal for running a boutique apiary. The Valley has an abundance of floral sources, a warm microclimate created by the river and there is an ever growing focus on high-quality, small-scale food and beverage businesses in the area – these are the things which inspired Tristan and Rebecca to start producing and selling high-quality honey. Their retail outlet in Launceston, Honey Tasmania, evolved not only as a way to share this delectable local honey, but also to help spread the word about the wonders of both honey and its maker: the honeybee herself.

It is generally considered that Nature's purest foods are also the healthiest and most flavourful. With this in mind, Honey Tasmania only offers honey which has been minimally filtered and heated. This leaves intact the full health benefits of the honey - vitamins, minerals, and enzymes, as well as its anti-bacterial properties - and of course, the full flavour.

The Tamar Valley and surrounding areas offer a wide range of flowers for the Campbell's bees to feed on, allowing for numerous pure varietal, single-floral honeys. During the Spring and Summer months, the bees feast on the nectar gathered from the blossoms of Manuka shrubs, Peppermint gums and the native Prickly Box, as well as the ever-present blackberries. In the new year, Tristan moves the hives further afield to harvest the world famous Leatherwood honey from the West Coast.

Honey can add many dimensions to your culinary creations, in much the same way wine does. Consider the versatility different honey varieties allow when coupled with food – distinctive tastes, aromas, textures and even colours which can inspire and delight when used to balance and enhance the qualities of the food. Clever use of different honeys can certainly add depth and interest to dishes, and not just the desserts!

tamar valley pantry
prickly box honey from honey tasmania

prickly box honey panna cotta
with rhubarb compote and chamomile sugared tuilé biscuits

ingredients

serves 6

100g Prickly Box Honey from Honey Tasmania
250g double cream
250g whole cream milk
6g gelatine leaves, titanium strength

1 chamomile tea bag
30g icing sugar
tuile biscuits (recipe pg 228)

method

Warm the cream, milk, and honey in a saucepan. Do not boil (boiling the cream and milk breaks the protein into small pieces). Stir with wooden spoon to dissolve.

Soak the leaves of gelatine in cold water. Squeeze all the water out of the gelatine before adding to the cream. Strain through a fine sieve into a bowl of simmering water, stirring occasionally til it has thickened like custard. Pour into 6 dariole moulds and set in fridge for 8 hrs.

To de-mould the panna cotta, tip the mould upside down and place a round-ended knife in the side to break the airlock of the plastic mould.

Mix the contents of the tea bag with the icing sugar and sprinkle on tuile biscuits to serve together with rhubarb compote.

rhubarb compote

ingredients

250g diced rhubarb, 3cm long
10g ginger, finely chopped
1 orange, zest only

65g caster sugar
½ vanilla pod, seeds only
50ml of sparkling wine

"Choose very young deep red stems of rhubarb for the best results"

method

Place all the ingredients in a saucepan and cook for about 15 minutes. Cool before serving.

honey + pistachio fudge

gluten free healthy fudge

ingredients

serves 8

2 tbsp Tasmanian Leatherwood Honey
350g dark coverture chocolate
250g natural peanut butter
150g pistachios
1 tbsp pure vanilla extract
¼ tsp sea salt

method

Melt the chocolate pieces in a pot on low heat. Remove and stir in the natural peanut butter.

Then add the pistachios, leatherwood honey, vanilla and salt flakes.

Mix together and spread into a deep cookie tray lined with paper.

Place in fridge for 2 hours until set.

Cut into squares. Makes approx. 28 small pieces

crystallized pistachios

ingredients

200g pistachios
200g caster sugar
150ml water

method

Pre- heat the oven 170°C. Place nuts on a tray and roast for 12 minutes.

Put water and sugar in a pot. Place on medium high heat to boil til temperature reaches 135°C or the syrup just starts to colour on the edges.

Add the pistachios and whisk until the syrup has completely caramelized and all the nuts have been coated.

Pour onto a baking tray lined with baking paper and allow to cool.

Nuts can be kept for up to 6 months in an airtight container.

tamar valley vineyards

josef chromy wines

Set amongst beautiful gardens with 100-year-old oak trees, Josef Chromy Wines' Cellardoor and Restaurant at Relbia is a stunning location. Overlooking a picturesque lake, winery and a 61-hectare vineyard that stretches for two kilometres along the hillside, the property is just a 15-minute drive south of Launceston and a five-minute drive from the Launceston Airport.

Originally an 1880's homestead, Josef Chromy Wines' Cellardoor and Restaurant recently opened a state-of-the-art function centre. The architecturally-designed building is sympathetic to the existing homestead and blends into the established old English gardens.

Overlooking the vineyard, the venue can accommodate 200 guests and is a superb location for weddings, conferences and events. Cellardoor offers a wide range of award-winning wines available for tasting and sale, including classic cool-climate varieties Sparkling, Pinot Gris, Riesling, Sauvignon Blanc, Chardonnay, Pinot Noir, Merlot, Botrytis Riesling and a Ruby Pinot Port.

Josef Chromy OAM has owned and developed some of Tasmania's leading wineries and Josef Chromy Wines is the culmination of his experience in the Tamar Valley. This shines through in the quality of the wines, food and hospitality offered at his cellardoor and restaurant.

The establishment has been included in the Top Cellardoors of Australia by such publications as Gourmet Traveller Wine and Australia Wine Business Magazine. The restaurant offers a superb a la carte menu, light meals, gourmet platters and desserts; all prepared by award-winning chef Sean Keating and his team.

tamar valley pantry
josef chromy sauvignon blanc

three cheese fondue
with josef chromy sauvignon blanc

ingredients

serves 6-8

450g gruyere cheese, grated
225g raclette cheese, grated
225g tilsit cheese, grated
15g cornflour
500g Josef Chromy Sauvignon Blanc
3 cloves garlic, whole

2 sprigs thyme
20g lemon juice
5g mustard powder
pinch ground cloves + white pepper

method

In a bowl mix the cheeses with the cornflour.
Bring the wine to a simmer over med- high heat. Remove from the stove.
Add thyme and garlic cloves. Infuse for 10 minutes then strain and allow to cool.
Bring the wine and lemon juice to the boil and add the cheese mix a handful at a time, whisking continuously until smooth and creamy.
Add the mustard, pepper and cloves. Stir until the mixture thickens.
Transfer into a fondue pot and serve with cornichons, bread and crudités of your choice.

"May be served with air dried beef prosciutto or just jardinière of vegetable "

tamar valley pantry
josef chromy chardonnay

rabbit cassoulet
with winter vegetables and chardonnay

ingredients

serves 4

2 wild shot rabbits, jointed in legs and saddle
500g duck fat, melted
sea salt + black pepper
1 bunch thyme
4 golden shallots, peeled
100g green beans, topped and tailed
8 brussels sprouts, cooked in chicken stock then cut in ½

baby carrots, peeled and cooked in chicken stock
2tbs tomatoes, skinned chopped and deseeded
4 whole garlic cloves, peeled and cooked in chicken stock
300ml chicken stock
200ml Josef Chromy Chardonnay
100g streaky bacon lardons, cooked crispy

method

In a large cryovac pouch, place the seasoned rabbit, melted duck fat and ½ the thyme. Seal and place in a sous-vide water bath at 75°C. Cook for 8-10 hours.

Remove and allow to cool before handling. Cut open the pouch and place the rabbit on a cooling rack. Cook brussels sprouts, baby carrots, and garlic cloves in chicken stock. Separate cooked vegetables from the stock and set both aside.

In a large skillet, brown the rabbit till golden. Remove from pan and keep warm. Do not wash the pan. Add the carrots, sprouts, beans, shallots and whole garlic cloves and caramelize. Place in the base of the serving dishes and keep warm.

In the same pan, de-glaze with the wine and add the chicken stock from the vegetables. Add tomatoes and reduce the mixture on high heat until it is a syrup like consistency.

Place the warm rabbit over the vegetables in the serving dishes and spoon the sauce ove.

Garnish with the bacon lardons and remainder of the thyme, then serve.

"As a chef, I like to be challenged with the finest ingredients Tasmania has to offer! Wild shot rabbit, together with this smoky wine, are two of the best -   Enjoy the ride!"

tamar valley pantry

landfall farm fresh

A value-adding venture promoting farm products has created a local, innovative, true, paddock-to-plate experience. Landfall Farm Fresh is a family owned and operated butchery and fresh food business established in 2008 by the fifth generation Archer siblings Ed, Will, Frank, Ellie and Mimi. Locally grown, premium quality, award winning products are offered, most notably Landfall Angus Beef and Landfall Prime Lamb.

The Archer family has farmed Landfall on the eastern banks of the Tamar River, north of Launceston, since 1876. Today Landfall and Greenhythe form the primary production operation where Landfall Prime Lamb and Landfall Angus Beef are grown. Landfall animals are farmed humanely, in a low-stress environment, within the strict guidelines of a quality assured program. Much time and research has been invested in the selection of genetics from around the globe to produce red meat products of the highest standard achievable. These products have been the key drawcard at the Landfall Farm Fresh retail outlet in Launceston.

A focal point of difference and invaluable business advantage is the close relationship between producer and retailer. This allows complete control of the supply chain, providing consumers with a guarantee of free range, grass fed and hormone growth promotant free products.

The face to face interaction between consumer and producer provides valuable learning for both parties. Consumer appreciation of product origin, product quality and education on cuts of meat and cooking methods has set a new standard of consumer satisfaction and awareness. A quote from a valued customer: "Families like you are the reason why my family moved to Tassie...I love buying 'real' food....especially from 'real' people".

The dedicated teams at Landfall and Landfall Farm Fresh are passionate and proud to provide consumers with positive eating experiences. Their locally grown, value for money and high quality products are consistently produced with integrity.

tamar valley pantry
landfall oyster blade steak

oyster blade steak tagliata

serves 4

ingredients

1 x 400g Landfall oyster blade steak
salt + pepper
a little olive oil
1 tsp dijon mustard
lemon, zest and juice
100ml extra virgin olive oil

1 tsp young rosemary needles, chopped
150g wild rocket
100g shaved grana padano or pecorino
4 garlic cloves, roasted in the skins, popped out and sliced
a little sea salt
8 white anchovies - optional

method

Depending on your preferred cooking method, prepare the bbq, frying pan, or hot plate - nice and hot.
Season the steak and brush with a little oil.
Bar mark the steak to give a crisscross effect.
Cook to your desired liking, then rest the steak in a warm place and prepare the rest of the dish.
Combine the mustard, rosemary, lemon juice and zest in a bowl then drizzle and whisk in the olive oil to form a emulsified sauce.
Cut the beef into servable pieces across the grain.
Sprinkle the wild rocket leaves on the serving plate. Place the beef over, then add the cheese, sliced garlic and the white anchovies, salt flakes and fresh ground pepper.
Drizzle with the mustard sauce and serve.

*"This particular cut of beef is recommended by the breeder - Trust him!
Full of flavour, it will be one of the most satisfying pieces of steak you will ever eat"*

tamar valley pantry
landfall lamb shoulder

pulled lamb noisette
with dutch cream potato rösti + savoy cabbage lamb broth

ingredients

serves 6-8

1 Landfall lamb shoulder, shank removed
seasoning: salt, pepper, caraway seeds and chopped garlic
200ml chicken stock (recipe pg 225)
4 medium dutch cream potatoes, peeled and grated

1 small onion, finely sliced and sautéd
60g gruyere cheese, grated
¼ savoy cabbage, finely sliced
1 tsp caraway seeds
4 cloves of garlic, peeled and roasted

method

lamb shoulder: Place in a cryovac bag with the seasoning and a little lamb or chicken stock then seal. Place in a sous–vide water bath cooker at 75°C for 12 hours. Remove the meat. Allow juices to cool, strain and reserve for later.

Remove all bones, sinew and fat from the meat so the lamb can be pulled apart.

Cover an A4 size sheet of foil with gladwrap with a 3cm overlap on all sides.

Form the shredded meat into a sausage shape on the gladwrap and roll tightly in the foil, twisting the ends together like a bon-bon. Completely chill overnight in the fridge.

potato rosti: Mix the potato, onion and cheese with some salt and pepper, then fry in non-stick frying pan with a little olive oil. Remove and form a small round ball, before replacing in the frying pan to cook and brown evenly. Place in an oven at 160°C to keep warm.

Remove the lamb from the fridge and cut quite thick noisettes with a serrated knife. Remove foil and gladwrap - it will not fall apart. Using the same frying pan, brown the lamb noisettes on both sides and place in the pre-heated oven 160°C for 15 minutes.

Heat the stock in a saucepan. Add some of the reserved cooking liquid for flavour. Add the cabbage and caraway seeds and pour into warm serving bowls.

Place the lamb noisette, which is now warmed through to 65°C, on top of the potato and place in the centre of the bowl. Garnish with the garlic cloves and serve.

"If you don't have a sous-vide bath (but I strongly recommend you get one !) - try a pot of water held at a temperature of 70°C."

leaning church vineyard

For a fresh, funky and fun approach to wine, whisky and cheese tasting, the multi-award winning Leaning Church Vineyard guarantees a truly unique experience.

Leaning Church is located in a spectacular natural amphitheatre at the foothills of Mount Arthur near Lilydale, 20 minutes from Launceston, in the internationally-acclaimed Pipers River wine region.

Established 24 years ago, the vineyard gained global recognition under the Lalla Gully and Clover Hill labels with premium Sparkling, Pinot Noir and Chardonnay, as well as a Sauvignon Blanc that has been declared one of the best in Australia.

Owners Sarah and Mark Hirst have developed a premium tourism, wine and food business at Leaning Church, including a wine, whisky and cheese tastings centre, a rustic cellardoor capable of seating up to 55, a permanent marquee on a fully-paved surface that can seat up to 140 for weddings and corporate functions, an historic "leaning" church perfect for weddings and dinner parties, and a new lakeside marquee site to seat up to 360.

With a focus on degustations and grazing feasts, our preferred caterers impress pre-booked groups with a focus on local produce, perfect presentation and service with a smile!

Visitors to Leaning Church can wander around the vineyard, relax on the boathouse deck, tour the "leaning" church, enjoy the landscaped herb and flower gardens, indulge in a glass of wine with a cheese plate, peruse local art, sample single malt whiskies and laugh at the quirky wine labels!

It's all about celebrating the best of Tasmania in a fun and interactive manner…

tamar valley pantry

leaning church sauvignon blanc

chicken + pistachio terrine
with apricot chutney

ingredients

serves 4

6 free-range chicken breast fillets ~ 150g ea
2 egg yolks
freshly ground white pepper
sea salt
450 ml double cream
½ bunch tarragon, chopped
100g dry roasted, peeled pistachio nuts
1 glass Leaning Church Sauvignon Blanc

apricot chutney

2 tbs garlic oil
2 banana shallots, diced small
250g frozen apricots
1 apple, peeled and diced
75g brown sugar
200ml cider or sherry vinegar
2 sprigs of fresh thyme

method

terrine: Cut 3 chicken fillets into small pieces and blend in a food processor for 1 min. Scrape down before blending again for a further minute. Place the whole bowl in the freezer for 30 minutes - this allows the chicken mixture to absorb the cream better in the next step.

Add the egg yolks and seasoning and blend again. Scrape down again before adding the double cream. While blending, pour a steady stream of wine til all mixed through. Fold the pistachio nuts and chopped taragon through the mixture and place the chicken mousse in a bowl in the fridge for 1-2 hours.

Slice the other chicken breasts into strips and seal in a non-stick frypan with a little olive oil til cooked but not coloured and chill down.

Pre-heat the oven to 180°C. Line the terrine dish with gladwrap and place a third of the mixture in the base. Layer the terrine with the chicken strips and then add more mousse, more fillets and mousse again, until all used up. Cover the top with foil and place in a water bath and bake for about 40minutes. Test with thermometer or skewer until the juices run clear. Remove from the oven and refrigerate for 12 hours. Serve sliced with a pot of the apricot chutney and a little dressed organic salad leaves.

chutney: In a saucepan, heat the garlic oil and fry off the shallots til just caramelized.
Add the sugar, thyme, vinegar, apricots, and apple and cook over a medium heat for about 30 minutes until it has reduced to the consistency of thick jam. Cool down.

"Great entrée picnic dish - can be made ahead of time so you too can relax and enjoy the day"

tamar valley pantry
leaning church vintage sparkling

warm strawberry salad
with granola, natural goats yoghurt and sparkling wine

serves 4

ingredients

375g strawberries, hulled and sliced
4 tbsp natural goats yoghurt
100g Tasmania granola
300ml Leaning Church Vintage Sparkling
150g sugar
mint leaves

method

Heat the sparkling wine with the sugar in a wide stainless fry pan.
Reduce the contents to a light syrup and add the strawberries for about 2 minutes. Remove strawberries from syrup to stop them cooking and cool immediately.
Divide the strawberries and syrup evenly into 4 soup plates and spoon a large tablespoon of the goats yoghurt in the middle.
Add the granola evenly over the 4 bowls.
Sprinkle with the baby mint leaves and serve.

"A sweet late picked Riesling would work as well
- but I would suggest reducing the sugar content by half"

home point, tamar riverr

lees orchard

Lees Orchard was planted in 1916 and was then purchased in 1939, just months before World War II, by Mr and Mrs Lees. They grew a range of apple varieties, including Jonathons, Croftons, Red Delicious, Cox's Orange Pippin, Granny Smith, Jonagold and Golden Delicious, as well as William, Packham and Beuree Bosc pears.

The couple started their family in a little hut on the orchard in 1940 and the family home was built in 1955.

Lees Orchard is still a family-run business but was signed over to Brendon and Karen Morrison in 2003. Extensive work has been carried out on the 11.3 hectare orchard with 80 per cent of the old style planting being removed and new styles being planted espalier style. New varieties include Pink Lady, Royal Gala, Fuji and Comice pears. All the original varieties are also still available.

Brendon, who has been working in orchards since he was 17, has brought his son Daniel into the orchard and they run the business together.

Lees Orchard recently planted six different varieties of cherries, which will come into production at the end of 2013. The future plan is to continue planting cherries and apples in the vacant ground on the property.

Lees Orchard is open to the public from the start of March until mid January. All varieties of apples and pears are available for purchase at the Orchard shed between Thursday and Saturday 9am to 5pm. Vegetables, cherries, quinces and figs are also available when in season. Lees Orchard is also at Launceston's Harvest Market each Saturday and at the Evandale market each Sunday.

tamar valley pantry
lees orchard pink lady apples

pink lady apple custard tart
serve with hellyer whiskey icecream

ingredients

serves 6

sweet pastry

180g butter, cut into cubes
250g plain flour, sifted
25g sugar
1 whole free range egg
1 free range egg yolk
salt pinch
1tbsp milk

filling

2 pink lady apples, cored, peeled and sliced
lemon juice
1 tbsp sugar
400ml thickened cream
4 free range egg yolks
60g caster sugar
vanilla essence

method

sweet pastry: Pre heat the oven 180°C

Put the butter, sugar, egg, egg yolk and milk into a food processor and blend till smooth.

Add the flour and salt. Mix together and form a ball. Wrap in plastic and place in fridge for about 2 hours.

Roll the pastry out thinly, cut the desired shape for your moulds, line with pastry then with baking paper and weight down with dried pulses, beans or coins. Replace in fridge for 20 minutes to avoid shrinking when being baked blind. Bake blind for 15 minutes then remove paper and beans and bake for further 15 minutes until golden.

filling: Place the apples with the sugar and lemon juice in a hot oven 220°C- 250°C for 10 – 15 minutes. Allow to cool.

Whisk the egg yolks, vanilla essence, sugar and cream together.

Place the cooked apples in the base of your tart shells.

Pour the cream mixture over and bake at 170°C until the filling is just set (approx. 20 minutes depending on the size of the shells). Remove, cool slightly and serve with icecream.

We suggest Hellyer Whisky Icecream. Garnish with mint optional

'Today you can buy some amazing ready-made pastry cases if time is an issue!"

tamar valley pantry
lees orchard beurre bosc pears

warm pear en croute
with chocolate honey sauce and cream

serves 4

ingredients

2 whole beurre bosc pears, peeled and cored with stalk intact
200g careme puff pastry

sugar syrup
500ml water
500g caster sugar
1 vanilla pod, split

chocolate sauce
200g dark chocolate
75g prickly honey
75g water

100g double cream

method

Pre heat the oven 200°C

Heat the ingredients for the sugar syrup in a large saucepan. When simmering, add the pears and cook until soft, then allow to cool down.

Draw a pear shape on thick paper and cut out a template.

Roll out the puff pastry until 1.5 cm thick then use the template to cut out the pear shape.

Place on a baking tray lined with baking paper and rest in the fridge for at least 30 minutes.

Cut the poached pear in half and place on top of the cut pastry.

Bake in the pre-heated oven for about 20 minutes until golden.

Prepare the chocolate sauce by heating the chocolate, honey and water, stirring until smooth.

Serve baked pear warm on the plate with a pool of the chocolate sauce.

Place a dessert spoon in a jug of warm water and then scrape a quenelle of double cream to serve on each plate.

"these ingredients are a match made in heaven!!"

lilydale larder

Lilydale Larder is the ultimate regional wine and food experience – located in the heart of the picturesque village of Lilydale only 20 minutes from Launceston.

Enjoy scrumptious home-baked sweet and savoury treats in the café, browse the Tasmanian providore, taste local wines, whisky, ciders and craft beer in the regional wine tasting bar, peruse the bottleshop, meet the locals in the public bar or celebrate your next function in the rustic room for up to 160 people.

Simple, elegant country food is beautifully presented in the café and providore – from locally-grown garlic, Tassie-roasted coffee, home-baked quiches over-loaded with Lilydale eggs, salmon sandwiches on rye to a full range of boutique-produced goods and crafts.
"It's just like walking into Auntie Joan's country kitchen where you are embraced by flour-ingrained hands, alluring home-baked smells, a fully-stocked pantry and a desperate desire to dip your finger in the mixing bowl," owners Sarah and Mark Hirst said!

"Relaxed good 'ole fashioned country hospitality ensures everyone is welcomed to their home away from home to relax, rejuvenate and replenish!"

Lilydale Larder also offers a wide range of special events – from local performers to national entertainers to local lamington cook-offs to wine appreciation courses to food, wine, cider,

whisky and craft beer tastings. And the small and large meeting rooms are perfect for weddings, parties, corporate meetings and celebrations.

The Meet the Producer Market in the Lilydale Larder carpark on the second Sunday of each month enables visitors to interact with fabulous stallholders, sample fresh produce, purchase captivating crafts and taste beautiful beverages.

Lilydale Larder is open seven days a week to tantalise your taste buds and overload your senses!

tamar valley pantry
free range eggs from lilydale larder

free range egg omelette
with swiss brown mushrooms, wilted spinach and raclette

ingredients

serves 1

4 free range eggs from Lilydale Larder
1 garlic clove, chopped
50g swiss brown mushrooms, sliced
20g butter

1 handful organic spinach leaves
40g raclette cheese, grated
salt and pepper
olive oil

method

Heat an omelette pan with a little olive oil.
Whisk eggs in a bowl. Set aside.
Fry the mushrooms and garlic in oil and half the butter. Set aside.
Without washing, add spinach leaves with remainder of the butter for 20 seconds and remove.
Add oil to the same pan and pour egg mixture, stirring until just formed on the base.
Add the cheese.
Fold into a perfect cigar shape.
Place on plate and slice a pocket down the centre.
Fill with spinach and mushrooms and serve.

"Lilydale Larder has great local, fresh free-range eggs available in store"

tamar valley pantry
goat chèvre from lilydale larder

chèvre tart

serves

ingredients

1 quantity shortcrust pastry (recipe pg 228)
2 handfuls english spinach, washed and stalks removed
2 tsp olive oil
1 brown onion, finely diced
1 clove garlic, finely chopped
1 handful each of silver beet and parsley, stalks removed
2 sprigs rosemary leaves, chopped
2 small sage leaves, torn into pieces
4 sprigs thyme, leaves only
900ml cream
2 bay leaves
salt and pepper to season
grated nutmeg to taste
120g goat chèvre
6 free range eggs (approximately 65g ea)

method

Line a high-sided, loose bottom 26-28cm tart tin with pastry and bake tart shell as per recipe.

Whilst pastry is baking, gently cook spinach in a covered pan with 2 tablespoons of water until soft. Press out all the water between paper towel, roughly chop and set aside.

In a clean pan, sweat the diced onion in the olive oil, covered, over a low heat, until soft but not coloured. Add the garlic and cook, then add washed silver beet, parsley, rosemary, sage, thyme and spinach.

In a separate pan, bring the cream to the boil with the bay leaves and a small pinch of salt, pepper and nutmeg. Add the onion and herb mix to the cream, return to the boil and taste for seasoning. Remove from heat and discard bay leaves.

In a large bowl, whisk the eggs well, then incorporate the hot cream mixture and pour into the tart shell. Crumble chèvre over the surface of the tart and bake at 180°C for 10 minutes, then reduce the temperature to 160°C and bake until set, about 20 minutes.

Remove from the oven and rest for 10 minutes before carefully unmoulding and cutting.

recipe supplied by lilydale larder

kings bridge, cataract gorge, launceston

tamar valley pantry

manubread

Producers of Fine Artisan Breads and Pastries, Launceston, Tasmania

The team at Manubread are passionate about producing the very best artisan breads and pastries. Their dedicated bakers are artists skilled in the traditions of French baking, producing a full range of sourdough, rye, and wholegrain loaves and baguettes, as well as a mouth-watering array of French pastries and brioche.

All their products are hand moulded and preservative free.

Manubread is a wholesale bakery and since their inception in 2012, have become Launceston's supplier of choice for artisan breads and pastries.

Manubread also retail direct to the public through the Launceston Harvest Market and the Evandale Market.

tamar valley pantry
manubread light rye

hot smoked ocean trout on rye

ingredients

serves 2

4 slices of Manubread light rye
hot smoked ocean trout
2 green zebra tomatoes, cored
25g organic salad leaves
1 tsp horseradish grated - mix with aioli
3 tbsp of aioli (recipe pg 50)

½ red onion
1 lemon
4 cornichons
½ bunch chives, whole
20g butter softened
cracked black pepper

method

Spread a little butter on the bread slices.
Place the salad leaves on the base of one of the slices and build your sandwich with the layers of salmon and sliced zebras. Drizzle with the aioli.
Season the sandwich with pepper, only in case salmon is a little high in salt.
Decorate with onion rings, cornichons, chive and lemon then serve.

"My version of the old Ruben sandwich with a definite Tassie twist"

tamar valley pantry
manubread fruit brioche loaf

sweet fruit brioche pudding

serves 6

ingredients

1 Manubread fruit brioche loaf, cut and sliced
3 free range eggs
3 tsp. caster sugar
1 vanilla pod, split and scrapped

50g butter, softened
250ml cream
250ml whole milk
1 tsp all spice

method

Pre heat the oven to 180°C.
Grease with a little butter 6 ramekin dishes and place on a baking tray.
Heat In a saucepan the cream, milk and vanilla.
Beat the eggs and sugar in a bowl, then add the all spice and warm milk to create a custard.
Soak the buttered slices of brioche in the custard.
Carefully add to the ramekins, then pour the remainder of the custard in the dishes.
Add warm water to the baking dish to form a water bath.
Place in the oven and bake for 25-30 minutes until golden and just set.
Serve immediately with your favourite icecream.

"This is an old fashioned winter favourite made with a classic French brioche"

nigel's gourmet on tamar

Nigel's Gourmet On Tamar is a family owned and operated business located in Exeter on the West Tamar Highway. Nigel purchased the butcher shop in 2005 after 10 years of working at the premises. A competition was held in 2007 to choose a new name and 'Nigel's Gourmet on Tamar' was born.

Tradition is of key importance at Nigel's Gourmet on Tamar so they practice the old-fashioned principles of buying local produce, free range and hormone free. They pride themselves in offering top quality produce along with ready-to-eat meals to make life simpler.

Utilising an on-site smoke oven, Nigel makes his own smoked Spanish chorizo, ham, bacon and cabana, as well as hot and cold smoked salmon. A range of smallgoods are also hand made on site, such as black pudding and pork kassler.

Producing more than 20 varieties of sausage each week, the team at Nigel's looks forward to tantalising your tastebuds with their extensive premium range.

Nigel's Gourmet on Tamar has been the recipient of Australian Meat Council Industry Award awards for:
- 2012 - Gold Medal Continental Sausage Class - Bratwurst
- 2011 - Winner - Tassie's Best Burger 'Pumpkin & Fetta'
- 2011 - Silver Medal Gourmet Sausage Class - Thai Green Curry Chicken & Prawn

tamar valley pantry
nigel's hot smoked salmon

hot smoked salmon risotto
with green peas and mini roma tomatoes

ingredients

serves 4

- 400g Nigel's Hot Smoked Salmon, flaked into bite size pieces
- a knob of butter
- ½ onion, finely chopped
- 1 garlic clove, finely chopped
- 200g carnaroli or aborio rice
- 2 bay leaves
- 100ml dry white wine
- 400ml fish stock (recipe pg 225)
- 80g peas, defrosted
- ½ punnet of mini roma tomatoes, cut in half and roasted
- 50g grated parmesan cheese
- 3 spring onion, sliced finely

method

Heat the butter in a saucepan over low heat and add the onion and garlic.
Sauté for 2 or 3 minutes until soft.
Add the rice and bay leaves. Continue to cook over medium heat for a further 2 or 3 minutes before adding the wine, stirring all the time.
Now add the warm fish stock a little at a time and continue to do so until all the stock has been used. Keep stirring - this will take approximately 30 minutes.
The risotto should now be creamy. Add the parmesan cheese, tomatoes, peas and half the salmon. Season to taste.
Arrange in warm serving bowls, placing the remaining salmon on top with spring onions and drizzle with chilli or basil oil.

"Because the salmon has been fully cooked in the smoking process you just need to warm through to serve. You can also add saffron threads or dill, or basil."

tamar valley pantry
nigel's chorizo sausage

chorizo sausage linguine
with chilli and sun blushed tomatoes

ingredients

serves 4

4 chorizo sausage, sliced on an angle
350g linguine durham wheat pasta
2 tbsp chilli oil (recipe pg 227)
1 large red onion, diced
2 fresh long chillies, chopped finely
200ml red wine (we suggest pinot noir)

120g sun blushed tomatoes, chopped
50g tomato paste
2 gloves garlic, chopped
fresh basil + parsley, chopped finely
sea salt and cracked pepper

method

Cook the pasta in a pot of salted water as per instructions on the packet.
Drain and keep warm.
Heat the chilli oil in a large frying pan. Add the onion, garlic and chillies and cook for 2 minutes.
Now add the sliced chorizo sausages and brown off in the pan before adding red wine, tomato paste and chopped tomatoes. Reduce and simmer for 15 minutes.
Season, then add the pasta. Stir through making sure the pasta is well covered by the sauce.
Finally, add the chopped herbs and serve in warmed pasta bowls.

"Another great dish for an easy entrée, brunch or eat by the couch dinner - and so quick!!

tasmanian poppy fields

tamar valley pantry
tasmanian poppy seeds

chick pea + vegetable curry
with poppy seed naan bread

serves 6

ingredients

naan bread
250g plain flour
2 tsp sugar
½ tsp salt
½ tsp baking powder
110-130ml whole milk
2 tsp vegetable oil
tasmanian poppy seeds
1 tsp melted butter

curry
1 onion, diced
1 clove garlic, chopped
100g cauliflower florets
1 celery stick, diced
½ small sweet potato, peeled and diced
15g curry powder
440g can of tomato, diced
440g can chick peas, drained
150ml vegetable stock
oil
salt + pepper
chopped coriander or chives
chilli, chopped - optional

method

naan bread
Pre-heat the grill plate.
Sift the salt, flour, sugar and baking powder in a bowl.
Mix the milk and vegetable oil together.
Make a well and add the wet ingredients to make a dough.
Knead for 10 minutes, and place in a warm spot covered with a damp tea towel.
Divide the dough into 6 even balls and roll out with a little flour into a teardrop shape.
Place the poppy seeds on the top. Then grill for 2-3 minutes on each side, brush with butter and serve hot.

curry
Heat the oil in a heavy based pan.
Add the curry powder and dry roast for 2 minutes.
Add the onion and garlic and sweat off for 3 minutes before adding the other vegetables.
Add the tinned tomatoes, stock and chick peas.
Cook through for approximately 20 minutes.
Add the chopped herbs and serve immediately with the warm naan bread.

"these world-class seeds are an important by-product of the Tasmanian Poppy Industry"

tamar valley pantry
tasmanian poppy seeds

seared tuna tataki
with japanese seaweed salad and wasabi soy

ingredients

serves 4

400g sashimi grade tuna, trimmed
1 fresh lime zest
1 tsp fresh finely grated root ginger
10g tasmanian poppy seeds
10g sesame seeds
1 egg white

1 tbsp peanut oil
100g japanese wakame seaweed salad
40g wasabi paste
40ml sashimi grade soy sauce
40g japanese mayo

method

Mix in a medium sized bowl, lime zest, ginger and all the seeds.
Brush the outside of the whole tuna piece with egg white.
Roll the tuna through the seed mixture.
In a hot skillet, heat the peanut oil on high heat.
Sear the tuna fillet around all the outside surfaces for 1 minute to form a crust.
Place on wire rack and rest.
Garnish the plate with a small amount of wasabi, seaweed, mayo and soy as shown.
Thinly slice the tuna being careful to cut through the crust then layer over lapping on the service plate.
Serve with garnishes.

"The crust works very well with beef or fish - try both sometime. Japanese wakame seaweed is available in Asian stores - often frozen"

ritual coffee

Ritual Coffee was founded in 2008 by Tim and Mel Jarosz, who were joined by roaster Stuart Grant in 2010. Since the beginning it has been something of a tumble-down the-rabbit-hole in search of quality coffee.

The first thing they discovered was that their raw ingredient – green coffee beans – needed to be fresh and of the highest possible quality.

"It's the same reason a restaurateur doesn't go trawling the supermarket for their vegies; if we want quality coffee, we need to know where it comes from, how it was grown, and who grew it," Tim said.

"That's why we partner with quality-minded producers and suppliers in long-term, mutually beneficial relationships. We pay well for great coffee," Mel added.

The second thing Ritual focuses on is roasting in a way that showcases the hard work of producer partners. They try to highlight the natural sweetness of a bean – notes of caramel, chocolate or brown sugar, depending on the coffee.

Then there is terroir. Each different region lends its character to the coffees grown there. Beans from the Yirgacheffe region in Southern Ethiopia can have a zesty fruit character; from

Nyeri in Kenya they are bright and lively; from San Agustín in Colombia they are sweet and buttery. "Our job as a roaster is simply to unlock these flavours," Tim said.

"Coffee is about people – from the millions of producers whose livelihoods depend on it, to the millions of coffee drinkers whose palates are thrilled by it every day.

"We're happy we could introduce the two of you!"

tamar valley pantry
ritual coffee

coffee parfait
with blood orange sauce and toffee nut clusters

ingredients

serves 10

8 free range egg yolks
100g caster sugar
100ml dessert wine botrytis or riesling
150ml of extra strong cold coffee
1 small pinch of cayenne pepper
300ml of whipped cream, soft peaks
1 tsp lemon juice

sauce
500ml blood orange juice
250g sugar
zest of 2 blood oranges

nuts
200g assorted roasted dry nuts, e.g. hazelnuts, almonds, pistachio
150g sugar
100ml hot water

method

"The parfait must be removed from the freezer at least 10-15 mins before you wish to serve. Very similar to a semi-fredo in texture for best results"

Prepare a loaf tin or cake tin lined with gladwrap and place in the freezer.

Whisk the egg yolks, sugar and dessert wine over a pot of warm water on the stove until light creamy and fluffy. Continue to whisk until the sabayon is at 80°C.

Remove from the heat and place the bowl over a large bowl of ice, continue to whisk until cold.

Add the cayenne and lemon juice and whisk one third of the whipped cream into the sabayon. Carefully fold the remainder of the cream with the coffee using a figure of 8 action. Pour into the lined mould and replace in freezer for up to 12 hours.

sauce: Place all ingredients into a pot on stove. Over a medium to high heat, simmer until all sugar is dissolved. Cool before using the syrup with the parfait.

nuts: Place in a heavy saucepan, sugar and water and boil til a golden caramel 180°C-182°C.
Place the pot in a bowl of ice water to prevent burning.
Pour over the nut clusters that have been placed on baking paper.
When cool, remove and set aside.
Pour a pool of the blood orange coulis on the serving plates.
Turn the parfait out onto a rectangular plate, cut slices or wedges out and place just off centre.
Garnish with the nuts and serve.

tamar valley pantry
ritual coffee

coffee crème brulée

serves 4-6

ingredients

450g double cream
150g whole full fat milk
3 tbsp ground coffee beans from Ritual Coffee
6 free range eggs yolks
50g caster sugar

method

Pre heat the oven 140°C.
Pour the milk, coffee and cream in a saucepan, place over heat and simmer.
In a bowl, whisk 10g of the sugar and egg yolks until pale and creamy.
Add a small amount of the coffee cream mixture into the egg and mix. Add the remainder slowly, mix well with a spatula not a whisk (see notes).
Strain the mixture through a fine sieve and pour into the moulds set for the oven in a water bath, making sure the water is 2/3 of the way up the dishes.
Cover with foil and bake for approx. 30 minutes til custard is set but still wobbles in the middle.
Take out of the bath and cool before placing in the fridge for at least 6 hours.
Just before serving, sprinkle with a thin layer of caster sugar and caramelise with a blow torch.
Serve immediately with coffee shortbread and coffee granita (recipes pg 146).

"Using a spatula avoids bubbles - if you have bubbles this will cause the caramelizing to burn very quickly. Remove the bubbles with absorbent kitchen paper before baking"

tamar valley pantry
ritual coffee

coffee shortbread

ingredients

serves 20 biscuits

- 175g plain flour
- ½ tsp baking powder
- 1 tsp salt
- 20ml strong coffee
- 90g butter, cold and cubed
- 100g caster sugar
- 40g egg yolk, beaten
- 35g olive oil
- sugar for dusting

method

Sift the flour, baking powder and salt in a bowl and set aside.

Using a mixer with a paddle, cream the butter and sugar till it becomes light and fluffy - about 5 minutes.

Reduce the speed to low and add the flour mix. Combine til the consistency of fine bread crumbs.

Combine coffee, oil and egg yolk and mix through until a dough is formed.

Wrap in plastic and place in the fridge for 2 hours.

Place the dough between 2 pieces of baking paper, roll into a rectangle approximately 5 cm thick and cut to fit the pastry into a tray 30 x 20 cm. Place in freezer for 20 minutes.

Pre-heat the oven to 150°C.

Remove top layer of baking paper and place tray in oven for 15-20 minutes.

Bake until golden brown. While still warm, using a palate knife, slide onto a board and cut into rectangles 3 x 5 cm. Sprinkle with sugar and cool.

coffee granita

ingredients

serves 4

- 60g ground coffee beans
- 600ml hot water
- 120g caster sugar
- mint leaves - optional

method

Place a shallow baking tray in the freezer to cool.

In a pot, mix hot water with coffee. Add the sugar and dissolve. Pour into frozen baking tray and place back into freezer. Once crystals have formed, draw a fork though and replace in freezer. Repeat every 40 minutes til all is done and you have crystals of coffee.

Place into a frozen glass ready for the assiette and serve.

"This should do the trick for a major coffee fix!"

147

alexandra suspension bridge, cataract gorge

rosevears waterfront tavern

Rosevears Waterfront Tavern is situated on the picturesque Tamar River in the heart of the Valley. This delightful historic tavern provides a unique waterfront dining experience with a mix of old world charm and fine fresh food.

Steeped in history, the Tavern was originally built by William Henry Rosevear back in 1831 on the current site at Cimitiere Point and named the "The Independent". This was a wooden structure and was first licensed back in 1831. In 1833, William changed its name to "The Half Way House" and again in 1835 to "The Rose Inn". In 1938 the hotel was completely destroyed by fire and later that year was re built, but this time with clay bricks, in a typical Georgian/Victorian style which is still at the core of the Tavern today.

Recently the historic Waterfront Tavern has undergone a major renovation and extensions in keeping with the traditional tavern atmosphere whilst bringing it back to its former glory.

You can still step back in time and have a beer in the locals bar, enjoying the open fireplace and stunning views. There is plenty of options to choose from with three function rooms, a cosy restaurant to relax in and the new large open air deck, all overlooking the Tamar River.

The tavern has a real focus on fresh local produce with the current owners breeding their own Black Angus at properties in Glengarry and Winkleigh. This beef is aged and placed straight on the menu at the restaurant, which has hearty meals with a modern twist. You can also experience great Tasmanian wines and local ales when you visit the Tavern. Future plans for the site include a vineyard/winery and accommodation.

The unique location provides a scenic journey to the Tavern. Whether you arrive by car, boat or helicopter the Rosevears Waterfront Tavern is the perfect destination for a relaxing meal, a cold drink and warm friendly warm service, all year around.

tamar valley pantry

tasmanian wallaby fillets
on roasted vegetables, wild rocket salad and red onion jam

serves 4

ingredients

450g tasmanian wallaby fillets
100g sweet potato, peeled and diced
100g parsnips, peeled and diced
1 packet Yorktown wild rocket
80g roasted cherry tomatoes
2 large red onions, sliced
2 tbsp garlic oil
100ml red wine
100ml balsamic vinegar
100g brown sugar
2 sprigs of thyme and rosemary
sea salt + cracked pepper
olive oil

a little chilli oil to serve

method

Add a little olive oil to a non-stick frying pan and fry off the vegetables to a nice golden caramel.
Place the vegetables in a pre-heated oven at 200°C for about 15 minutes or until soft.
In a saucepan, heat up the garlic oil and fry off the red onion til just caramelized.
Add the sugar, thyme, rosemary, wine and balsamic vinegar and cook over a medium heat for about 30 minutes until reduced to the consistency of thick jam. Cool down.
Brush the wallaby fillets with olive or flavoured oil of your choice, season with sea salt and pepper and place on a pre-heated hot BBQ.
Sear on both sides - remember that 3-4 minutes will probably be enough depending on the thickness of the meat.
Take off the heat and rest for at least 5-10 minutes. Slice and drain on kitchen paper.
Mix through the salad ingredients and roasted vegetables in a large bowl, drizzle with a little chilli oil and pile in the centre of a serving bowl.
Arrange the wallaby on top and then place a spoon of the jam on top and serve.

"Such an under used meat - so lean, so flavoursome! but most of all so easy to prepare"

char grilled veal rib eye
with five spice butter and roasted kipflers

serves 12

ingredients

5 star anise
½ tsp whole cloves
1 tsp whole fennel seeds
1 tsp szechuan peppercorns
1 tsp ground cinnamon
salt flakes
unsalted butter

char grilled veal rib eye,
    cooked medium rare and wel rested
roasted kipflers
corn on the cob, grilled

method

Grind all the spices, except the cinnamon and salt flakes, in a spice grinder.
Combine with salt, cinnamon and butter and blend til evenly distributed.
Place on baking paper to form a long sausage and roll into a cylinder and then refrigerate till needed.

Serve with your favorite steak, cooked to medium-rare and well rested with a side of roasted kipflers and grilled corn on the cob.

When cooking steak it is vital to let it rest for at least 5-10 minutes to allow the juices to settle.

"you can keep the butter frozen for up to 6 months or the spices in an airtight container for 3 months"

tamar valley truffles

Tamar Valley Truffles is Tasmania's largest privately-owned trufferie, growing world-class Black Perigord truffles.

They are commonly referred to as `black gold' – the highest quality product purchased by renowned chefs from across Asia and Australia for up to $2500/kilo. Feedback from chefs, including a 3-star Michelin Restaurant, suggests that Tamar Valley Truffles provide a premium product, rivalling the best from Europe.

Tamar Valley Truffles firmly believes that the consistency of its offerings is a result of being based in the beautiful Tamar Valley and the hard work and dedication of an extremely professional and passionate team.

But before gastronomes around the globe can enjoy the earthy and subtle sensation, there is a long production process involving patience and precision. Three thousand deciduous and evergreen oak trees were planted at the family farm located on the beautiful Trevallyn Dam in 2000. It took five years before the first prized delicacy was discovered.

Between June and September each year, highly-trained dogs locate the ripe truffles, which grow in the ground as a result of a symbiotic relationship with the tree roots that

have been inoculated with the truffles spores (Tuber Melanosporum).
The truffle has been etched into European folklore as a revered item. Tamar Valley Truffles is proud to raise its profile in Tasmania, through the inception of the inaugural Tasmanian Truffle Festival, which will continue to evolve and expand each year.

Tamar Valley Truffles also looks forward to continuing to grow its relationship with the best chefs from across Tasmania, Australia and around the world.

tamar valley pantry
tamar valley truffles

potted duck + truffle jelly

serves 4

ingredients

4 duck legs
4 juniper berries
6 star anise
2 cinnamon sticks
6 black peppercorns
2 bay leaves
1 sprig of thyme
zest of ½ orange + ½ lemon
60g salt

500g duck fat
2 sprigs of rosemary
4 cloves of garlic, peeled

40g Tamar Valley Black Truffles
400ml beef consommé
3 titanium sheets of gelatine, soaked in cold water squeezed dry

method

Dry roast the juniper berries, star anise, cinnamon, peppercorns, thyme and bay leaves then grind in a spice grinder.

Mix the zests and spices together with the salt and rub on the duck legs. Cover and leave overnight to infuse.

Pre-heat the oven to 75°C.

Rinse and pat dry the duck legs and place in a casserole dish. Melt the duck fat and pour over the legs. Add 2 sprigs of rosemary and the cloves of garlic.

Place in the oven for 18 hours.

Remove the legs and allow to cool at room temperature. Blitz the fat and cooking juices and set aside.

Warm the consommé and add the gelatine before pouring into the ramekins 10cm thick. Now add the truffles cut into fine strips.

Place in a fridge until set.

Shred the flesh of the duck using 2 forks and add a small amount of the fat just to bind.

Divide the meat into the ramekins, press down firmly and reset in fridge for about 40 minutes.

Place the ramekins in a bowl of very hot water for 30 seconds, remove and turn on to serving plate.

Serve with charred bread.

"A classic combination of flavours - duck and truffles are made for each other."

tamar valley pantry
tamar valley truffles

truffle consommé en surprise

serves 6-8

ingredients

50g Tamar Valley Truffles
100ml dry sherry or madeira
1 litre of strong beef stock

200g puff pastry
1 egg

clarification

3 egg whites, whisk gently til foamy
3 egg shells
250g lean beef mince, (97% fat free topside)
sea salt
150g in total of diced leek, onion, celery, carrot in a food processor but do not puree

method

Slice the truffles very fine, reserving the best 2 slices per serve and add to the sherry to infuse until needed. The smaller pieces can be added to the stock to impart flavour.

In a mixing bowl, mix the vegetables, salt, mince beef, and egg shells together before adding the whisked egg whites.

Mix thoroughly for 5 minutes.

Put the stock in a large saucepan and mix through the clarification. Place on the stove on medium heat and using a large whisk, keep the clarification from sticking to the bottom of the pot. As soon as the stock becomes hot, stop using the whisk and turn to simmer.

From now on, do not stir the stock. Let the clarification (or raft as we know it) float to the top. Through a crack in the raft, you will be able to see the clear amber liquid below.

Allow to cool before removing the raft, then strain the stock through a coffee filter, large muslin or clean chux.

Place the 2 slices of truffle in each ramekin and fill with the consommé.

Roll out the pastry to 5cm thick and cut discs to cover the ramekins with an overlay. Brush the edge of the ramekin with egg wash and seal the top with the disc of pastry. Glaze the top and place in the fridge for at least one hour before use.

Place the consommé bowls on a baking tray, evenly spaced and place in a pre-heated oven at 220°C for 15-20 minutes until golden. The pastry will form a magical dome and you need to serve quickly.

"This dish has the wow factor - get it right and the room fills with the perfume of truffles.

To have a room full of these golden domes impresses most people - even Prince Charles and the late Princess Diana to whom I served it in 1981"

nighttime in the tamar valley

tasmanian hotel and catering supplies

Tasmanian Hotel and Catering Supplies (formerly Tasmanian Hotel and Club Supplies) was established in 1980 to service the hospitality industry in Tasmania. The locally owned and operated business was purchased by Robert Dutton, Brad Dutton and Craig O'Brien in 2010 and has grown to be the state's leading source of hospitality supplies.

THCS stocks and distributes thousands of items used in the hospitality industry and also sells directly to the public. With showrooms in Launceston, Devonport and Hobart, the company offers an extensive range of commercial and retail products, both on site or accessible by order.

Some of THCS' major projects and key customers in the last two years include the fit-out of Woolworths' Distribution Centre's staff canteen, the supply and fit-out of the kitchens and accommodation areas of Barnbougle and Lost Farm Golf Courses, and the Agritas new learning project in Smithton.

The company supplies to most of Tasmania's leading restaurants, cafes, hotels, motels and bakeries, including the luxury Saffire Freycinet hotel, MONA (Museum of Old and New Art), the Good Stone Group, and Stillwater.

It is also the preferred supplier of catering supplies to Federal Hotels and Grand Chancellor Properties.

Employing more than 30 Tasmanians across the State at the three sites, THCS is committed to providing quality products and service to all its customers. From commercial operators to members of the public looking for something for the home, THCS has what you need and more.

"These ingredients work so well together!

crispy pork belly
with john's asian sauce

serves 6

While it might seem like a lot, the method is very straight forward. Rewarding to both you and your guests. Also allowing some sauce left over for next time - keep sealed in the fridge for about 3-4 weeks

ingredients

pork
1kg free range pork belly, bone in
½ tsp all spice
3 cloves
2 star anise
1 tsp coriander seeds
1 tsp five spice
sea salt
vegetable oil
2 tbsp ground nut oil or grape seed oil

john's asian sauce
2 tbsp chilli oil (recipe pg 227)
½ red onion, finely chopped
2 garlic gloves, chopped
¼ stick lemon grass, finely chopped
1 cm piece of ginger, finely chopped
3 star anise
2 red chillies, chopped
1 bunch coriander, root + stalk only
150g palm sugar
250ml light soy
3 tbsp fish sauce
100ml water
30ml dark mushroom soy
150ml char sui sauce
¼ bunch spring onion, sliced on angle

method

Pre-heat the oven to 75°C.

Score the skin of the pork with a very sharp knife.

Dry roast the spices and grind in a spice grinder and mix with the salt and oil, then rub all over the pork belly.

Place in the oven on a rack in a baking tray with a little water in the bottom. Cover with a lid or foil.

Remove after 12-14 hours, take away the lid and allow to cool completely before cutting away the bones. At this point try not to eat the meat from the bones- I said try!

Prepare the sauce - In a medium saucepan, add the chilli oil and gently fry off all the onion, garlic, lemon grass, ginger, star anise, chillies and coriander.

Now add the palm sugar, soy, fish sauce, water, char sui, and dark mushroom soy. Heat slowly then reduce by about ¼. Add spring onion and allow to cool.

Pre heat your hooded BBQ or heavy based non-stick fry pan and when hot, add a little nut oil or grape seed oil. Place the pork belly skin side down on a flat plate or frying pan on a high heat and maintain until the skin is crispy. Remove pork belly, cut and serve with the dipping sauce, steamed rice and maybe some baby bok choy.

lamb primal rump roast
with herb mustard crust on puy puy lentil ragout

serves 4

ingredients

2 lamb rump primal, fat removed
sea salt + cracked pepper
vegetable oil

crust

1 tsp each of sage, thyme and rosemary, finely chopped
1 tbsp seeded mustard
1 tbsp tomato concasse -(garlic onion tomato cooked down to a sauce)

100g puy puy lentils, pre-cooked in boiling salted water for 30 minutes and drained
½ onion, diced finely
1 glove garlic, chopped
100ml lamb jus
1 tbsp rosemary, chopped

method

Pre heat the oven to 180°C.

Season the lamb rumps and seal in a hot skillet with a little vegetable oil all over the surface.

Remove and place in a baking tray and place in the pre-heated oven for approx. 20 -25 minutes.

Remove and rest for a further 10 minutes in a warm place on a cooling rack.

Mix together in a small bowl, the herbs, seeded mustard, and tomato concasse ready to top the lamb rumps.

In a saucepan, reduce the jus with the chopped rosemary and the cooked puy puy lentils.

Serve the lentils on a warm serving platter.

Smear the crust on the lamb, then slice and place over the warm lentils.

"It's very important to rest the meat once removed from the oven to avoid the release of valuable juices and to keep the meat moist. If you are unsure of how cooked the meat is - use a meat probe. A core temp of 55°C will give you medium rare or pink"

tamar valley pantry

the mill providore and gallery

The Mill Providore and Gallery showcases Tasmania's fine foods, art works and Tasmanian handcrafted gifts. Proprietors Susannah Torcasio and Denis Visentin offer a warm welcome and an intimate knowledge of the products of the Tamar Valley region.

The Mill Providore and Gallery is located on the top two floors of an historic 1830's flour mill on the banks of the picturesque Tamar River, above Launceston's acclaimed Stillwater River Cafe, Restaurant & Wine Bar, near King's Bridge - the beginning of the scenic walk to Launceston's iconic Cataract Gorge.

On the first floor above the restaurant you'll find a wide variety of mouth-watering local produce in the delicatessen featuring artisan cheeses, smallgoods and Tasmanian seafood. The Mill showcases the best of Tasmanian producers including jams and preserves, relishes, olive oils, nuts, locally roasted coffee, culinary lavender, local spices, honey and hand-made chocolate and fudge. A quality selection of Tamar valley wines, craft beers and ciders is also on offer.

The Mill is the perfect place for gifts, especially handmade arts and crafts – including jewellery, pottery, ceramics, textiles and hand-made knits. Also featured is a wide selection of wood design utilising Tasmania's unique timbers crafted by local artisans – including sassafras, Huon pine, myrtle and blackwood. The Mill is the perfect place to

find a unique gift, or something special for yourself.

Upstairs the contemporary art gallery features Tasmanian artists with new exhibitions every month. The gallery presents works in a range of mediums from paintings, drawings and photography to sculpture, textiles and furniture design.

173

tamar valley pantry

native pepperberries from the mill providore

"this dish uses a native species of the Tasmanian bush - the pepperberry"

seared wild hare's loin
with brussels sprouts, mushrooms + native pepperberry sauce

serves 4

ingredients

4 wild shot hare loins, ends removed, centre cut only
olive oil
200g brussel sprouts, peeled and crossed at the base with a knife
50g butter
sea salt
cracked pepper
150ml full bodied red wine
250ml game jus
20g freeze dried Tasmanian Native Pepperberries, ground
2 golden shallots
200g of mixed mushrooms, (oyster, shitake, swiss brown)

method

Season the hare loins with a little ground native pepperberry and brush with olive oil. Bring to room temperature.

Steam the brussel sprouts for 10-15 minutes in a steamer before placing them in a small casserole dish with a lid with cubes of butter and seasoning.

Place in a pre-heated oven at 200°C for a further 10-15 minutes.

In a saucepan reduce the red wine by 2/3 before adding the game jus.

Add the native pepperberry at the end when you have a syrup like consistency. Keep warm.

Heat a large non-stick frying pan. Add a little olive oil and when hot, sear the hare loins all the way round.

Turn the heat down to medium and add the mixed mushrooms, cooking for 3-4 minutes. Remove from the pan.

Place warm potato mash on 4 warm serving plates.

Place the mushrooms in a cluster some of each variety along with the brussels sprouts.

Slice each loin into 3 before arranging on the mash and pour the game jus around on each plate and serve.

Unlike air-dried berries, freeze-dried retains the floral fragrance and also the amazing colour inside the skin of the berry - very bright purple pigment. By adding at the last minute and not heating you retain these qualities -you can actually smell the bush in the fruit! A must for all culinary buffs"

tamar valley pantry
tasmanian sloe gin from the mill providore

sloe gin cheesecake

ingredients

serves 8

base
8 chocolate digestive biscuits, crumbed
3 tbsp caster sugar
100g butter

jelly
75ml Sloe Gin
75ml blackcurrant and apple juice
50g caster sugar
2 leaves of titanium gelatine sheets, pre-soaked

cheesecake
400g mascarpone
150g icing sugar
50ml Tasmanian Sloe Gin
1 lime, juice and zest
600ml double cream, soft whip
2 leaves of titanium gelatine, pre-soaked in cold water

method

base: Melt the butter in a saucepan and add the biscuit crumbs and sugar. Whilst warm, press in the base of the moulds you intend to use. Place in the fridge for about 1 hour.

jelly: Heat in a saucepan, the sloe gin, blackcurrant and apple juice, sugar and add the squeezed out leaves of gelatine until dissolved. Bring to room temperature.

cheesecake: Melt the gelatine in sloe gin and lime juice. Cool slightly.
Mix together the lime zest, icing sugar and mascarpone before adding the melted gelatine mixture then folding through the soft peaked whipped cream.
Pour evenly into the moulds with the biscuit base leaving approximately 2 cm for the jelly. Place in the fridge for 2 hours to set before poring the jelly on top. Replace back in the fridge for 2 hours before serving with a Tasmanian Sloe Gin shot and a slice of fudge.

"The natural colour of the sloe berries makes for a great colour as well as flavour"

chocolate + orange fudge

serves 6-8

ingredients

250g dark chocolate
250g natural peanut butter

2 tbsp tasmanian honey
1 tsp vanilla essence

1 tsp orange zest
2 tsp Cointreau

method

Melt the chocolate in saucepan over low heat. Add the natural peanut butter, honey, cointreau, zest and vanilla. Pour into a shallow baking tray and refrigerate overnight. Slice a thin piece for each guest.

178

tamar valley pantry

trevallyn grocer

The Trevallyn Grocer was established in 2006 by Marcus Douglas and his partner Jo McBain. It was born out of a wish to have a store that was a purveyor of fine food items produced locally, in Australia and from overseas. Many hours were spent strolling through delicatessens and markets in Melbourne and Sydney for inspiration.

Trevallyn is a wonderful older suburb, nestled against the magnificent Cataract Gorge and its bushland surrounds, with amazing views across the Tamar River. The Trevallyn Grocer is only a three-minute drive from the Launceston CBD and is conveniently located across the old Gorge Bridge en route to the Cataract Gorge grounds and Trevallyn Recreation area.

The Grocer has an in-house delicatessen supplying local smallgoods, local and imported cheese and fresh seasonal produce, such as plump Tasmanian scallops and Tassal and Huon Atlantic salmon. Fruit and vegetables are restocked daily, the meat cabinet is filled with produce from local suppliers and butchers, and the dairy case showcases some of the best local milk, yoghurts and cheese.

An extensive range of Tasmanian wines, ciders and beers are also stocked here. Herbies spices, organic lines and their gluten free range are other items that make the Trevallyn Grocer an exciting place to shop.

The Trevallyn Grocer is a convenient place to stock up for picnics, for tourists staying in self contained apartments, and locals who want something the bigger supermarkets don't offer.

And if you sampled something on your trip around Tassie and wished you had more to take home, there is a good chance they have it here or can get it for you.

tamar valley pantry

tasmanian scallops from trevallyn grocer

tasmanian scallops
with buckwheat noodles, kaffir lime, wasabi + ginger butter

ingredients

serves 4

160g soba noodles
400g fresh tasmania scallops
salt + ground white pepper
a little olive oil
1 fresh lime, zest and juice
1 grated kafier lime flower,
    or thinly sliced kaifer lime leaf

25g pickled ginger, chopped
a squeeze wasabi paste
100ml double cream
80g butter, hard, diced
100ml fish stock, hot
½ packet micro herbs

method

Heat a frying pan or skillet.
Blanch in salted water, the soba noodles, drain and keep warm.
Flash fry off the seasoned scallops in a splash of oil then remove. Do not wash the pan.
De glaze with the fish stock. Add lime juice, zest, kafier lime, ginger, wasabi and finally cream.
Bring to the boil, reduce, then whisk in the hard knobs of butter removing the pan from the heat.
Place the scallops in the sauce to re heat off the stove.
Arrange noodles on a warm plate. Place the scallops around and spoon the sauce over each scallop.
Garnish with the micro herbs and serve.

"Once the butter is added do not reduce further to prevent the sauce from splitting"

tamar valley pantry
boerewors sausage from trevallyn grocer

boerewors sausage
sauerkraut, mustard and mrs ball's relish

serves 2

ingredients

1 whole boerewors sausage, approx 450g
½ savoy cabbage, cut into strips
1 tsp juniper berries
500ml apple juice
1 tsp caraway seeds
1 tbsp salt
1 tbsp sugar

50ml white wine
½ tsp black peppercorns, cracked
½ white onion, finely sliced in half ways
50g speck

serve with

40g dijon mustard
50g mrs ball's relish

method

Sauerkraut: Place the cabbage in a large saucepan, sprinkle with salt and leave for about 2 hours - this is part of the souring effect.
Squeeze the cabbage dry.
Fry off the speck in a little oil. Caramelise, then add the onion, wine, apple juice, caraway seeds and sugar. Bring to the boil, then add the cracked pepper and juniper berries. Simmer 30 minutes.

Grill the boerewors sausage on the grill or BBQ. Keep warm.
Place the condiments, including the sauerkraut, in small bowls.
Serve immediately with the sausage.

"Sauerkraut can also be purchased in a can or cryovac pouch if you wish"

van dieman brewing

Established in 2009, Van Dieman Brewing is a family owned and locally operated craft brewery, nestled amongst century-old English Oak trees just outside the historic northern Tasmanian town of Evandale.

Van Dieman brews with dedication, passion and hard work, utilising Tasmania's pristine natural resources. All beers are crafted from only the freshest ingredients, most grown within Tasmania.

Van Dieman Brewing is dedicated to delivering fresh, progressive and unique beers directly to you, in the process unveiling some of the world's classic beer styles. The beers are completely natural, do not undergo filtration or pasteurisation, and are 100 per cent preservative and additive free.

Owner Will Tatchell not only focuses on producing some consistently terrific beers, but he likes to have a bit of fun through experimentation and ingredients perhaps not normally associated with beer production. Through the new Mash Up series of beers, Will continues to evolve and push the boundaries of beer experimentation through a collection of collaborative brews with local Tasmanian primary producers.

Beers, such as the barrel-aged sour ale, Hedgerow, have been internationally recognised as being a world-class example of this ground-breaking style. A portion of this beer spends time in French oak barrels and is aged on a combination of Rose hips, Sloe and Hawthorn berries – all sourced from hedgerows on the brewery property.

Van Dieman Brewing - We Do Real Craft Beer.

187

tamar valley pantry
van dieman dubbel shot beer

slow cooked pork hock
with van dieman dubbel shot beer

ingredients

serves 2

2 fresh free range pork hocks
1 x 500 ml Van Dieman Dubbel Shot Beer
250ml chicken or beef stock
4 gloves garlic, peeled
3 star anise
1cm piece of ginger
3cm piece of lemon grass
sea salt + pepper

method

Place the pork hock in a cryovac pouch along with the star anise, lemon grass, ginger, garlic and beer then seal.
Place the pouch in a sous-vide machine pre-set at 75°C for 12 hours
Once removed, cool slightly so you can handle the pouch and carefully remove the hocks and set aside.
Place the juices in a saucepan, and chill rapidly in the freezer.
Remove from freezer and dispose of the fat that forms at the surface.
Place back on the stove at a very high flame to reduce the liquid that has now jellied. Add the stock and reduce further till you have syrupy like sauce. Strain and season ready to serve.
In this case, I have chosen kale as an accompaniment but you can use mash, rice or vegetables if you wish.
Place in warm serving bowl and place the warm hock alongside pouring the sauce over and around the dish.

"The dubbel shot beer with its sweet chocolate and rich hazelnut flavours of the coffee and bready malt characters of the beer go so well with pork - try it you will be amazed!"

tamar valley pantry

van dieman stacks bluff stout

short cut beef ribs
with van dieman oatmeal stout marinade and sauce

ingredients

serves 2

450g short cut beef ribs, bone in
330ml bottle of Van Dieman Stacks Bluff Stout
1 whole onion, diced
2 garlic clove, diced
sea salt + cracked pepper
vegetable oil

60ml beef jus
500g kenebac potatoes, peeled
300g butter
240g whole milk
1tsp horseradish cream
sea salt + ground white pepper

method

Season the beef ribs with the salt and cracked pepper and place in a cryovac bag with stout, onions and garlic. Seal and place in a sous-vide water bath set at 75°C for 12 hours.
Remove, and once slightly cooled, strain the juices and skim the fat off and reduce by at least half.
Add the beef jus and keep warm.
Prepare the potatoes by cutting into even pieces. Place the potatoes in a steamer and cook for 30 minutes at just under steam. Drain then rinse under cold water.
Bring a fresh pan of water to the boil, add the potatoes and cook until soft and falling apart.
Drain the potatoes and dry in a hot oven for 5 minutes.
Remove and put through a potato ricer, add the butter and beat vigorously. Add the warm milk with the horseradish and season with salt and ground white pepper. Keep warm.
Flash fry the ribs on a heated BBQ to caramelise the outside of the meat.
Serve the potatoes in a warm small bowl, drizzle some of the sauce on the serving plate before placing the short ribs.

"Great dish to share with someone special
- have it with lots of the wonderful sauce."

jacob's ladder, ben lomond

vélo wines

Welcome to vélo. If you love food, wine, art and life in general, this is the place for you!

There is an energy about us that sets us apart. It's a shared passion for creating beautiful things with our own hands. At vélo you can meet the person who made the wine, painted the painting, designed the building and grew the food.

The ambience at vélo is very special. Set on a vineyard in a peaceful rural setting, the outdoors comes in through huge glass windows, the sky scape is dynamic and the restaurant is awash with natural light. Each wall tells a story, with photos, paintings and memorabilia showcasing the vélo story.

Our staff members are young, vibrant and knowledgeable. We taste, create and live our 'vita vélo' with passion and care, and our customers are just part of the family.

At the heart of our restaurant is a huge wood fired oven, providing traditional wood fired pizza, slow roasted meats and everything else we can get in there. We have a strong focus on seasonal local produce.

At the rear of the winery are three large terraced garden beds where we grow fresh herbs and produce for our restaurant.

There is a strong European theme to everything we produce at vélo, a reflection of the influence of over a decade of living, learning and loving the cuisines of France and Italy.

We hope we can provide you with a wonderful experience, great memories and some little vélo souvenirs to take home. Enjoy!

tamar valley pantry
vélo cabernet

roasted venison medallions
with beetroot, horseradish mash and vélo cabernet sauce

ingredients

serves 6

- 1 piece of fallow venison topside - approx 800g
- olive oil
- 2 golden shallots, diced very fine
- 2 gloves of garlic, diced very fine
- 150ml vélo Cabernet wine
- 250ml venison jus
- kenebac potatoes, peeled
- 1 tsp horseradish cream
- 300g butter
- 240g whole milk
- 300g organic beetroot
- sea salt
- ground white pepper

method

Scrub beetroot and wrap in foil and bake for 90 minutes. Once done, peel and cut into wedges.

Prepare the potatoes by cutting into even pieces. Placing the potatoes in a steamer, cook for 30 minutes at just under steam. Drain then rinse under cold water.

Bring a fresh pan of water to the boil, add the potatoes and cook until soft and falling apart.

Drain the potatoes and dry in a hot oven for 5 minutes. Remove and put through a potato ricer, add the butter and beat vigorously. Add the warm milk with the horseradish and season with salt and ground white pepper. Keep warm.

In a saucepan, add the golden shallots and garlic with a little olive oil. Fry until soft, then add the red wine and reduce by ¾, then add the jus and reduce again by half. Keep warm.

Season the venison with a little garlic oil, salt and cracked pepper.

Seal off in a very hot skillet evenly on all sides before placing in a hot oven 220°C for approx 15-20minutes. Remove from the oven and rest in a warm place for 5-10minutes.

Spoon the potato mash on the serving plates and place the beetroot evenly around the plates.

Cut the venison against the grain and drain on kitchen paper before placing on the warm plate. Add the jus and serve.

"Venison is a great meat to work with - if treated right it can give you great results! Because of its very lean qualities it does not need a lot of cooking"

tamar valley pantry
vélo white wine

pizza de fruits de mere

ingredients

serves 4

4 Pizza bases
    or
300g plain flour
2 tbsp olive oil
70-100ml water
Mix together to form a dough and roll out 4 evenly shaped bases making sure to dock the pastry brush with a little olive oil

sauce
2 tbsp olive oil
1 onion, finely chopped
1 garlic clove, finely chopped
200g tinned tomatoes, diced
pinch of sugar, salt & pepper
1 tsp italian herb

topping
8 large king prawns
80g smoked salmon
80g flathead fillets
80g fresh ocean trout fillets
16 large black lip mussels
80g peeled prawn meat
120g egmont cheese
20g white anchovies
60g baby clams
1 tbsp fresh basil, shredded
chilli oil - optional

method

Pre- heat the oven to 230°C

sauce: Heat the oil, sweat off onions and garlic. Add the tomatoes, sugar, seasoning, and herbs and reduce for 3-4 minutes on medium heat. Cool down.

Once cool, spread a little of the sauce on each of the bases.

topping: First sprinkle one third of Egmont cheese on the bases, then slowly add the remainder of the seafood ingredients.

Sprinkle the remainder of the cheese evenly on top.

Place in the oven on a pizza tray 8-10 minutes. Check the bases are cooked - you may wish to slip the pizza onto the floor of the oven to finish off.

Drizzle with chilli oil and fresh basil, then cut and serve with a glass of vélo white wine.

"Ideally, pizzas are best cooked in a wood fired pizza oven on a stone floor if you have one - if not a good cook can always improvise!"

autumn in brickfields park, launceston

tamar valley pantry

westhaven dairy

Award-winning Westhaven Dairy began life as a dairy goat stud farm run by Geoff and Lorraine Mance in the late sixties, located in the rich fertile Tamar Valley region of Northern Tasmania.

Over the years the stud evolved from being a small supplier of goat's milk to becoming a manufacturer of quality specialty Tasmanian cow and goat milk yoghurts and cheeses.

Westhaven began manufacturing in Launceston in 1993, sourcing its milk from farms located in the clean environs of Northern Tasmania and producing award-winning quality products that are synonymous with small Australian boutique dairy manufacturers.

The business continues to grow and evolve at the behest of market demands and Westhaven imagination; making products as diverse as soft and subtle French style cheese (Chèvre) to Paneer for the Indian restaurant market.

Westhaven produces award-winning goat and cow yoghurt; silky and creamy varieties. They also produce Goat Chèvre and Fetta, in both flavoured and marinated varieties; and Cow Fetta, Paneer, Quark and Haloumi.

Westhaven Dairy has received many Gold, Silver and Bronze awards from 1998 to 2013 from the Royal Agricultural Society of Tasmania Wrest Point Hobart Fine Food Awards with its crowning achievement coming in 2012. Of the 14 products entered that year, 13 won medals, including six gold. Goat Natural Yoghurt won Champion of its class and Natural Chèvre was Reserve Champion.

The staff at Westhaven Dairy take great pride in producing handmade quality products that reflect the best produce that Tasmania has to offer.

tamar valley pantry
westhaven paneer cheese

palak paneer

serves 4

ingredients

225g Westhaven Paneer, cubed
2 bunch baby spinach
1 tsp cumin seeds
1 tsp fenugreek seeds
pinch garam marsala
2 tsp vegetable oil
1 onion, finely chopped
2cm piece of ginger, finely chopped
4 cloves garlic, peeled and chopped fine
2tbsp thickened cream
sea salt
200g tinned tomatoes, chopped
2 fresh chillies, sliced - optional
1 tbsp coriander, chopped

method

Blanch the spinach leaves in a little salted water and refresh in cold water before squeezing dry, then puree until smooth.
Dry roast the spices and grind in a spice grinder.
Heat the oil in a frying pan, then add the ground spices,
onions, garlic and ginger and fry till golden.
Add the chopped tomatoes, cheese, cream and at the last minute, the puree spinach.
Stir until the cheese is hot and pour into a warm serving dish.
Garnish with chopped coriander and chilli (optional) and serve with rice and/or roti bread.

"This is a well-known Indian dish. The secret to keeping the dish bright green is to add the spinach at the end so the colour remains vibrant"

tamar valley pantry
westhaven goat chèvre

roasted beetroot + chèvre salad
with orange and balsamic dressing + toasted walnuts

serves 8

ingredients

2 bunches of local beetroot
1 orange, juice and zest
2 tbsp. balsamic vinegar
1 clove garlic, minced
½ tsp fresh thyme
3 tsp olive oil
150g Westhaven Goats' Chèrve, crumbed
80g toasted walnuts
1 packet wild rocket
salt + pepper to taste

method

Cut the stalk of the beetroot leaving 2.5cms on the stem.
Wrap the beets individually in foil and roast in a hot oven at 200°C for about 1 hour.
Cool immediately, then peel and cut into wedges.
Place in a bowl.

dressing

In another bowl, combine garlic, orange zest and juice, thyme and balsamic vinegar.
Slowly drizzle in olive oil while whisking continuously.
Season to taste.

Place the rocket in a serving dish.
Place the beetroot over and sprinkle with crumbled goats' cheese, then spoon over dressing.

Top with toasted walnuts and serve

"you can use the beetroot whilst still warm"

"Great combination of Westhaven Chèrve, beetroot and of course Tassie walnuts – fresh, dry and sweet."

209

tamar valley pantry

wild fish

The Tamar Valley is centred on one of the major rivers in Tasmania, and being no more than 40 minutes away from the coast means that the opportunities to catch your own fish are abundant.

World famous brown and rainbow trout can be caught in some of the most pristine trout waters of the world, and there is a dazzling array of salt water fish that can be found around the coast. With Blue Eye Trevalla, Australian Salmon or the best tasting flathead available, wetting a line, from either a boat or from the shore is almost guaranteed to produce a feed.

If you are going after trout, you will need to obtain a fishing licence from Service Tasmania or your local tackle shop. The same goes for the use of gill nets and if you are thinking of catching crayfish or abalone for dinner.

The great thing about Tasmania is that all of these species are readily available. A few hours off one of the many jetties on the Tamar River, or a short dive on the East Coast should see you dining like a king.

poached blue eye cod
in saffron + tomato essence with dutch creams

ingredients

serves 4

4 x 180g blue eye cod fillets, de boned and skinned
500ml fish stock (recipe pg 225)
1g Tasmania saffron, infused in 30ml of fish stock before use
250g dutch cream potatoes, peeled
1 onion, finely sliced
1 baby fennel, finely sliced
6 vine-ripened tomatoes, blanched, seeded, peeled and cut in slithers
sea salt
ground white pepper

method

Par-boil or steam the dutch creams for about 20 minutes depending on the size of potatoes, then cool before cutting in wedges.

Fill a saucepan with warm fish stock. Add the saffron threads.

Season the fish fillets with salt and pepper before placing in the simmering fish stock to poach until just cooked or soft to touch. Keep warm.

Reduce the fish stock a little, then add onion and fennel. Simmer for 5 minutes, then add the cooked potatoes and tomato slithers.

Drain and divide the vegetables equally into 4 warm bowls.

Place the fish on top of the vegetables and pour the warm stock around and over the fish.

"Locally known as Trevalla, this fish is looked upon as one of Tasmania's finest deep water fish. Flavoursome, meaty and firm make it perfect for this dish. You could enrich the dish with a small amount of aioli on top should you wish"

tamar valley pantry
local jack mackerel

smoked fish kedgeree
using local jack mackerel

ingredients

serves 6

500g local jack mackerel, smoked, flesh only, de-boned and skinned
300g basmati rice
½ onion, finely diced
2 cloves of garlic, finely chopped
55g of butter
1 tbsp madras curry powder
freshly grated nutmeg
300ml milk

200ml water
150ml double cream
sea salt + cracked pepper
½ bunch chopped parsley

garnish

hardboiled eggs, halved
a good pinch of cayenne pepper
fresh lime or lemon cheeks

method

Melt the butter in a saucepan and gently fry the onion and garlic till soft.
Combine the nutmeg, curry powder and rice into the pot.
Add the milk and cream along with water.
When the rice comes to the boil, add the fish pieces (reserve a small amount to garnish).
Continue cooking til the rice is soft. You may need to adjust the liquid so the rice doesn't become too dry.
Season to taste. Garnish with reserved fish, boiled egg, chopped parsley and lime cheeks.

"This makes a great brunch dish for the weekend on the Tamar"

ye olde green grocer

When Andrew and Garth were persuaded by wives Lisa and Jeanette to give up careers in commercial fishing and pursue a different line of work, no one expected that they would end up becoming vegos!

The ex-market garden that they bought in Dilston had been operating since the Second World War and was the start of a very successful operation to supply fresh fruit and vegetables to the Launceston market.

Today the Ye Olde Greengrocer on Charles Street is as important to the Launceston public as any retail outlet. Over the years they have developed a reputation for having the best produce in town. Their clean green, pesticide free policy has been an important way of differentiating themselves from the rest.

Having the biggest range of produce has always been important, and their customers know that along with the extensive range, is a clear knowledge of where the food comes from, how it was produced and how it can be best used.

While fresh Tasmanian produce is a vital aspect of this business, with products such as Yorktown Organics fine range of organically grown produce always in stock, they also source seasonal fruit and vegetables from around the country. So if you are looking for the best of tropical summer fruit like mangos or pineapples, Ye Olde Greengrocer is the place to visit. They also stock a wonderful array of other local produce such as honey, preserves, and oils.

Stocking the best of local and nationally produced fruit and vegetables this family run, home grown business is really worth a visit.

tamar valley pantry

mushrooms from ye olde green grocer

smoky mushroom mélange
with garden herbs, crispy bacon and warm bread

ingredients

serves 4

400g assorted mushrooms: shitake, swiss brown, chestnut, oyster or wild mushrooms
sea salt + cracked pepper
1 tsp smoked paprika
½ red onion, finely sliced
olive oil
1 bunch garlic chives
½ glass of dry white wine

3 rashers of bacon, grilled crispy

herb butter
1 tsp italian parsley, chopped
½ tsp sage, chopped
½ tsp rosemary, chopped
100g butter, softened

method

Cut the mushrooms evenly into chunks, except the small oyster mushrooms which you can leave whole. Set aside.
To make herb butter, mix together the butter and all herbs except the garlic chives.
Place in a small piece of baking paper and roll into a sausage shape, place in the fridge til set.
In a large skillet, heat some olive oil and the red onion. Cook till soft without colour.
In a bowl, toss the mushrooms in smoked paprika and seasoning.
Add the mushrooms to the skillet keeping the heat turned up, then deglaze with the wine.
Add ½ the herb butter. Take off the heat and swirl the pan around until the butter is melted and has formed a sauce.
Now add the garlic chives and serve in a pre-warmed dish. Garnish with crispy bacon and warm bread.

*"This simple dish is for mushroom lovers
Reminds me of foraging in the forest of Europe as dawn breaks
to see last nights' bounty. If you are vegetarian, omit the bacon"*

tamar valley pantry

vegetables from ye olde green grocer

pumpkin + baby spinach salad
with balsamic and nigella seed dressing

serves 4

ingredients

500g butternut pumpkin, peeled and diced into small cubes
2 tbsp vegetable oil for roasting
1 pkt baby spinach leaves
1 red onion, sliced finely
red capsicum, diced finely
1 tsp garlic, chopped fine
1 chilli (optional)
sea salt
cracked pepper
3 spring onions, finely sliced

dressing
125ml olive oil
50ml balsamic vinegar
10g of nigella seeds

method

In a large frying pan, heat the vegetable oil and add the cut pumpkin.
Brown slightly and place in a pre-heated oven at 200°C for 15- 20 minutes, until soft.
Set aside and allow to cool till just warm.

dressing

Put the oil, seeds and balsamic vinegar in a small glass jar or bottle and shake to mix well.

Mix the onion, capsicum, chilli, garlic and baby spinach leaves together and add the pumpkin pieces.
Now gently coat with the dressing.
Season to taste before serving with sliced spring onion on top.

"Always mix the salad at the last minute to avoid soggy leaves and to make sure your salad is alive and fresh"

cook's notes

All ingredients used in this book have be purchased locally or produced in the Tamar Valley.

In most recipes I use Sea Salt Flakes.

I refer to pepper as cracked, ground white or just freshly ground black and white. For mash, fish, poultry and white sauces, I would use ground white.

Always taste the food and correct the seasoning to suit.

Olive oil for salads, marinades or drizzles should be extra virgin.

All eggs used in this book are free range, farm eggs from down the road with a bit of s---t on them. That's just fine - it's what's inside that matters. The yolks from real free range chooks are amazing - I know, ask my wife - we have had turkeys, geese, guineau fowl, 4 varieties of ducks, as well as chooks.

Included in this book are recipes for various types of stock, however good quality pre-made stocks are available from local suppliers.

To make a jus, reduce good quality stock on high heat by at least half until it is the consistency of thin gravy.

Spoon measurements are level measuring spoons - 5ml liquid equals 5g for solids as a rule.
Weights have been stated in kilograms and grams.

Oven baking temperatures are always given in Celsius. This always has to be approximate, as cooking times will vary with equipment and ingredients. You have to do a little bit of judging for yourself - it's what makes us better cooks.

Where the exact time is crucial, the time will be stipulated.
Generally I use a range - cook for 8-10 minutes or till golden brown.
I have often said that cooking is not hard, but the timing of everything being ready together is like an orchestra all in sync.

Do wash all vegetables and salads prior to preparing and cooking.

Sous-vide means cooked under vacuum. This machine or water bath cooks at a specific temperature and time and results in minimal weight

loss and also retains all the cooking juices. Ingredients are always sealed in a vacuum sealed pouch.

Cryovac or vacuum sealed is achieved by placing the product in a bag and removing most of the air using a specialist machine to prolong the shelf life.

Thermomix™ is a specific cooking apparatus that can chop, grind, heat, and blend.
I use a digital probe to check internal temperature of cooked meats

Careme brand Puff pastry is a fantastic product which saves plenty of valuable time and is readily available.

Sloe gin - made from the sloe berry giving a fantastic deep rose colour.

Boerewors Sausage - a South African speciality sausage.

Mrs Balls Relish - a south African relish which is readily available.

Gelatine - I use only Titanium strength leaf. Much easier and more accurate. Always soften in cold water and squeeze excess water off before use.

Char Sui Sauce - a sweet hoisin sherry honey and vinegar flavoured sauce found in Asian stores.

Freeze dried raspberries - available from some health food shops and of course Cocobean.

Chocolate Couverture - very high quality chocolate rich in cocoa butter, readily available from delicatessens and providores.

Paneer - goats style of Fetta used in Indian cuisine.

One final word, always buy local whenever possible, support the producers, give them feedback, and above all enjoy this book and as always...

Happy Cooking

John

kitchen essentials

chicken and beef stock makes 1.7 litres

ingredients

stage one
- 4kg chicken carcass
- 1 pig's trotter (2kg), split
- 2 carrots, diced
- 2 onions, diced
- 2 celery sticks, diced
- ½ head fennel, diced
- 2 tablespoons tomato puree
- 2 cloves garlic

stage two
- 200g shin of beef, diced
- 1 turkey thigh, diced
- 2 carrots, diced
- 1 celery stick, diced
- 1 onion, diced
- 150ml red wine
- 100g tinned tomatoes
- 1 sprig thyme

method

Preheat the oven to 220° C.
Trim the chicken carcass of unwanted fat. Place in a roasting tin.
Roast to a golden brown. Do not burn the bones or a bitter flavour will occur.
Place the pig's trotter in a large pot (ideally a tall narrow pot – best for stocks).
Add vegetable (not garlic) from 'stage one' to the roasting tin.
Return to the oven and allow the vegetables to brown, stirring from time to time, approx 30 minutes.
Once vegetables have caramelized and browned, add tomato puree and stir into the vegetables.
Deglaze the tin with approximately 2 litres of cold water.
Mix well, scraping the bottom of the tin with a wooden spatula. Add bones to the pot.
Cut the garlic cloves in half and add to the pot. Top up with water leaving 5cms of bones showing above the water level (they will shrink as the stock cooks).
Bring to the boil. Reduce to a gentle simmer and cook for 2 ½ hours. Skim the surface occasionally.
Strain the stock into a clean pot.
Using a large frypan, brown the diced meat and vegetables from 'stage two. This may need to be done in small quantities to avoid stewing the meat.
Add the browned meat and vegetables to the stock. Deglaze the frying pan with red wine.
Add stock along with the tomatoes and thyme. Return to a simmer, skimming off scum as it appears.
Cook the stock at a gentle simmer for a further 2 hours. Strain the stock through a sieve into covered containers.
Cool then remove any fat from the surface.
Store in the fridge for up to 48 hours or freeze for later use.

chicken stock makes 1.3 litres

ingredients

- 3 chicken carcasses, remove skin and fat
- 1 leek, cut into quarters
- 2 celery sticks, halve lengthwise
- 1 large carrot, quartered
- 1 onion, leave skins on and quarter
- 1 small head of garlic, halved across its equator
- 6 peppercorns
- 1 bay leaf
- 1 sprig thyme
- 3 tsp of parsley or tarragon stalks

method

Place carcasses in a pot large enough to be half full with the bones.
Just cover bones with approximately 2.5 litres of cold water.
Bring to boil, then reduce heat to simmer.
Using a large spoon, skim the fat and scum from the surface of the stock.
Add the remaining ingredients over the carcasses.
Allow to simmer very slowly, skimming any scum or fat again.
The simmering stock will rise and fall through the vegetables, acting as a filter, absorbing the refuse from the liquid leaving it crystal clear. Leave to simmer like this for 2-3 hours.
Taste regularly until you notice the flavour stops improving – it's now ready.
Remove the pot from the heat and empty the stock into a colander placed over a bowl.
Pass the stock through a fine sieve into a 2.5 litre container or jug.
Cover and allow to cool by placing in a sink of cold water. When cool, place in the fridge overnight.
Skim off any fat that settles on top.
Spoon out the now jellied stock into tubs. This can be frozen until ready to use.

fish stock makes 1.2 litres

ingredients

- 1kg fish frames including heads (eg. blue eye or snapper broken in smaller pieces)
- 1 tbsp olive oil
- 1 onion, finely sliced
- 1 small leek green top
- 2 sticks celery
- 2 tops of fennel
- 1 bay leaf
- parsley stalks
- 1 glass dry white wine

method

Soak the fish frames in cold water for 10 minutes.
In a small stock pot, heat the olive oil before adding the vegetables, peppercorns and bay leaf.
Cook without colour.
Add white wine and reduce by half then add the fish frames.
Cover with 1.5 litres of water and bring to the boil. Skim off any impurities that come to the surface and simmer for about 20 minutes then turn off the heat.
Let stand for 3-4 hours before passing through a fine strainer and skim again.
Refrigerate before using - this should jelly overnight. The jellying of any stock is the good sign of a great stock.
The clarity will depend on how well you have removed all the impurities.

marinated vegetable stock
makes 1.2 litres

ingredients
- 1 large onion
- 1 leek
- 2 celery sticks
- 1 head of fennel (optional)
- 4 large carrots
- 1 head of garlic, halved across its equator
- 8 peppercorns, crushed
- 1 tsp coriander seeds
- 1 star anise – optional
- 1 bay leaf – optional
- 40g mixed fresh herbs
- 300ml white wine

method

Chop all the vegetables into 1cm pieces. Place in a pot and cover with water.
Add the garlic, peppercorns, coriander seeds, star anise and bay leaf.
Bring to boil, then simmer for further 10 minutes.
Add the fresh herbs and simmer for a further 2 minutes.
Add the white wine and remove from the heat.
Leave covered and allow to marinate for 48 hours in a cool place.
Once marinated, strain the stock through a fine sieve.
Ready to use immediately or you can freeze it for up to 6 weeks.

basil pesto

"This is called the handful recipe - it's so easy"

ingredients
- 1 garlic glove
- 2 handfuls of basil leaves
- 1 handful pine nuts, toasted
- 1 handful of grated parmesan
- lemon juice and olive oil
- sea salt and cracked pepper

method

Place the garlic with a little salt in the mortar and pestle and pound to a paste.
Transfer the garlic into a food processor, add the basil and pine nuts and blend to a smooth paste.
Add the parmesan cheese, blend again adding a little lemon juice and streaming in the olive oil until you have a thick, double cream consistency. Add a little pepper and check seasoning.

balsamic syrup

ingredients
- 1 bottle balsamic vinegar

method

Bring the balsamic vinegar to the boil and simmer until reduced by half.
Leave to cool. Ideally store in a squeezy bottle for convenience.

chilli oil makes approximately 1 litre

ingredients
200g ripe red chillies
850mls sunflower oil

method
Slice the chillies in half lengthwise and place in a saucepan. Add oil and bring to the boil.
Simmer gently for 5 minutes. Remove from the heat and allow to cool (approximately 2 hours).
When cool, transfer the chillies and oil to a plastic tub with a lid.
Store in a cool place for 2-3 weeks.
Pour oil through a sieve to remove the chillies before using (this will stop the oil from becoming too hot).
Store in a bottle for up to 3 months. Ensure you label as chilli oil so it's not confused with other oils.

herb oil makes approximately 300mls

ingredients
85g mixed fresh chives, parsley and tarragon
300ml olive oil

method
Put the herbs into a pot of heavily salted boiling water for 10 seconds – this sets the chlorophyll and keeps them green, giving the oil a rich colour.
Drain and refresh under cold running water to stop the cooking process.
Wring dry in a clean tea towel. Chop roughly.
Put the herbs into a liquidizer with the oil and blitz for 3 minutes until the oil is emulsified and green.
If having difficulty with the herbs releasing their colour, tip oil into a small saucepan and bring to the boil over a low heat – this should fix the colour.
Cool immediately and store in a squeezy bottle in the fridge.
Will keep up to 10 days – will start to lose its colour after this. You can also freeze the herb oil.

garlic oil makes approximately 300mls

ingredients
1 head of garlic
300ml olive oil

method
Peel garlic and place in bottle with good quality extra virgin olive oil. Allow to infuse.
The longer the better.

tamar valley pantry

crème patisserie
"Crème patisserie is to chefs what concrete is to builders"

ingredients
serves 6

- 4 whole free-range eggs
- 65g caster sugar
- 15g plain flour
- 15g cornflour
- 350g full cream milk
- 1 vanilla pod split seed, scrapped out
- Icing sugar for dusting

method

In a large bowl, whisk the eggs and sugar till they turn very pale.
Whisk in the cornflour and plain flour and set aside.
Place the milk and vanilla in a heavy bottomed sauce pan. Heat to simmer stage.
Pour slowly over the egg mixture, whisking all the time and return all to saucepan.
Bring back to the boil, stirring all the time with a wooden spoon. Cook for 1 minute.
Scrape into a clean bowl and dust with icing sugar to stop skin forming.

tuile biscuits
"These biscuits are perfect for delicate desserts such as panna cotta"

ingredients
makes 12

- 115g butter
- 115g icing sugar
- 115g plain flour
- 1tsp vanilla essence
- 3 free range egg whites, lightly whisked

method

Pre-heat the oven 180°C.
Beat the butter and sugar in a mixer until very smooth, fluffy and pale colour. Fold in the flour, egg whites and vanilla before placing in the fridge for 1 hour.
Lay a template of your chosen shape over baking paper and using a palate knife, spread mixture over.
Bake for 5-10 minutes or til crisp and golden. Remove from the oven and while still warm you may wish to shape them and dust with the chamomile sugar. Cool before serving.
These biscuits are perfect for delicate desserts such as panna cotta or various ice creams and sorbets.

shortcrust pastry
makes 1x28cm tart shell or 6-8 small tartlets

ingredients

- 240g plain flour, sifted
- ¼ tsp salt
- 180g cold unsalted butter, 1.5cm dice
- 60ml ice cold water

method

Sift the flour and salt onto a clean bench. Add diced butter and mix together with a knife. Add ice cold water then lightly knead till dough just forms. Wrap in gladwrap and refrigerate for only 20 minutes.
Roll dough on a floured work bench to approximately 5mm thickness. Roll pastry off the rolling pin over your tart tin leaving approximately 1.5cm of pastry above the rim of the tin. Fold this excess pastry back over the rim of the tin. Prick the bottom of the tart shell all over with a fork. Cover completely with foil and place in freezer for 20 minutes. Preheat oven to 190°C.
Remove tart shell from the freezer, line with greaseproof paper, then fill with baking weights or dried beans and blind bake for 10 minutes. Reduce the temperature to 170°C, remove weights and greaseproof paper and continue cooking until pastry is crisp and light caramel in colour. Remove from oven.

suppliers listing

BILAMBIL BERRY FARM
Kent and Alyssa Mainwaring
270 Pipers River Road Turners Marsh, TAS, 7267
p: 0417 317 229
e: bilambil@gmail.com

blueberry clafoutis   22

blueberry + pink grapefruit sorbet   24

BRIDESTOWE LAVENDER ESTATE
296 Gillespies Road Nabowla, TAS, 7260
p: 03 6352 8182
e: info@bridestowelavender.com.au
w: www.bridestowelavender.com.au
Open: September to April 9.00am - 5.00pm Daily
           May to August 10.00am - 4.00pm Mon - Fri

lavender chicken   28

lavender + honey icecream   30

COCOBEAN CHOCOLATE
Theresa Streefland
82 George Street Launceston, TAS, 7250
p: 03 6331 7016
e: enquiries@cocobeanchocolate.com.au
w: www.cocobeanchocolate.com.au
Open: 9.00am - 5.00pm Monday-Friday
        9.30am - 2.00pm Saturday

chocolate torte   34

white chocolate brownie   38

CORONEA GROVE OLIVES
Rob and Jen Goddard
121 Saunders Drive Hadspen, TAS, 7290
p: 03 6393 7856
e: rpgoddard@bigpond.com
facebook.com/CoroneaGroveOlives

salmon + fennel carpaccio   42

blue eye cod romesco   44

231

FOUR SPRINGS PRODUCE
Annette and Nevil Reed
338 Four Springs Road Selbourne, TAS, 7292
p: 03 6396 6160
Annette 0438 009 522   Nevil 0438 866 160
e: anreed@harboursat.com.au
w: www.fourspringsproduce.com

tomato + fennel tart   48

roasted purple stripe garlic aioli   50

GOATY HILL WINES
Natasha Nieuwhof
530 Auburn Road Kayena, TAS, 7270
p: 1300 819 997
e: info@goatyhill.com
w: www.goatyhill.com
Open: 10.00am - 5.00pm Daily

bbq quail   56

mussel broth   58

HARVEST FARMERS' MARKET
Cimitiere Street Car Park
Launceston (opposite Albert Hall)
p: 0417 352 780
e: info@harvestmarket.org.au
w: www.harvestmarket.org.au
Open: 8.30am – 12.30pm every Saturday
          All year round - rain, hail or shine!

duck confit   62

thai beef salad   64

HILLWOOD FARMGATE
139 Hillwood Road Hillwood, TAS, 7252
p: 03 6394 8092
e: info@meandervalleydairy.com.au
w: www.meandervalleydairy.com.au

strawberry millefeuille   68

strawberry flambe   70

HONEY TASMANIA
Rebecca and Tristan Campbell
22 Quadrant Mall Launceston, TAS, 7250
p: 03 6331 9300   m: 0438 570 719
e: honey@honeytasmania.com
w: www.honeytasmania.com
Open: 10.00am - 4.00pm Monday-Friday
            10.00am - 2.00pm Saturday

prickly box honey panna cotta   76

honey + pistachio fudge and
crystallized pistachios   78

suppliers listing continued

tamar valley pantry

JOSEF CHROMY WINES
370 Relbia Road Relbia, TAS, 7258
p: 03 6335 8700
e: wine@josefchromy.com.au
w: www.josefchromy.com.au
Open: 10.00am - 5.00pm Daily
          Dinner Friday and Saturday from 7pm

three cheese fondue   84

rabbit cassoulet   86

LANDFALL FARM FRESH
Ed, Will, Frank, Ellie and Mimi Archer
49 Balfour Street Launceston, TAS, 7250
p: 03 6334 5751
e: orders@landfallfarmfresh.com.au
w: www.landfallfarmfresh.com.au
Open: 10.00am - 5.30pm Thursday - Friday
          9.00am - 2.00pm Saturday

oyster blade steak tagliata   92

pulled lamb noisette   94

LEANING CHURCH VINEYARD
Sarah and Mark Hirst
76 Brooks Road Lalla, TAS, 7267
p: 03 6395 4447
e: info@leaningchurch.com.au
w: www.leaningchurch.com.au
Open: 10.00am - 5.00pm Daily Oct 1 to Apr 30

chicken + pistachio terrine   100

warm strawberry salad   102

LEES ORCHARD
Brendon and Daniel Morrison
161 John Lees Drive Dilston, TAS, 7252
p: 03 6328 1158
e: bmorrison_leesorchard@hotmail.com
Open: 9.00am - 5.00pm Thursday - Saturday
Harvest Market: 8.30am - 12.30pm Saturday
Evandale Market: 8.00am - 2.00pm Sunday

pink lady apple custard tart   108

warm pear en croute   110

LILYDALE LARDER
Ian White
1983 Lilydale Road Lilydale, TAS, 7268
p: 03 6395 1230
e: info@lilydalelarder.com.au
w: www.lilydalelarder.com.au
Open: 7 days a week

free range egg omelette   116

chèvre tart   118

MANUBREAD
215 Invermay Road Invermay, TAS, 7248
p: 03 6326 8848
e: info@manubread.com.au
w: www.manubread.com.au
Harvest Market: 8.30am - 12.30pm Saturday
Evandale Market: 8.00am - 1.00pm Sunday

ocean trout on french rye	124
sweet fruit brioche pudding	126

NIGEL'S GOURMET ON TAMAR
Nigel Birrell
Main Road Exeter, TAS, 7275
p: 03 6394 4215
e: nigelsgourmet@gmail.com
w: www.nigelsgourmet.com.au
Open: 8.00am - 6.30pm Monday - Friday
           8.00am - 1.00pm Saturday

hot smoked salmon risotto	130
chorizo sausage linguine	132

RITUAL COFFEE
6/31a Churchill Park Drive Invermay, TAS, 7248
p: 0429 314 206
e: tim@ritualcoffee.com.au
w: www.ritualcoffee.com.au

coffee parfait	142
coffee assiette	144

ROSEVEARS WATERFRONT TAVERN
215 Rosevears Drive, Rosevears TAS 7277
p: 03 6394 4074
e: info@rosevearstavern.com.au
w: www.rosevearstavern.com.au
Open: 7 days a week

tasmanian wallaby fillets	152
char grilled veal rib eye	154

TAMAR VALLEY TRUFFLES
Marcus Jessup
PO Box 698
Riverside, TAS, 7250
p: +61 417 112 655
e: marcus@tamarvalleytruffles.com.au
w: www.tamarvalleytruffles.com.au

potted duck + truffle jelly	158
truffle consommé en surprise	160

suppliers listing continued

tamar valley pantry

164 TASMANIAN HOTEL & CATERING SUPPLIES
Craig O'Brien, Robert and Brad Dutton
3-5 Merino Street Kings Meadows, TAS, 7249
p: 03 6344 5588
e: office@tashotel.com.au
w: www.tashotel.com.au
Open: 8.00am - 5.00pm Monday - Friday
       9.00am - 1.00pm Saturday

crispy pork belly 166
lamb primal rump roast 168

172 THE MILL PROVIDORE AND GALLERY
Susannah Torcasio
Ritchie's Mill 2 Bridge Road Launceston, TAS, 7250
p: 03 6331 0777
e: info@millprovidore.com.au
w: www.millprovidore.com.au
Open: 8.30am - 5.30pm Monday - Friday
8.00am - 5.00pm Saturday, 9.00am - 4.00pm Sunday

seared wild hare's loin 174
sloe gin trio 176

180 TREVALLYN GROCER
Marcus Douglas, Jo McBain
Cnr Gorge Rd & Osborne Ave Trevallyn, TAS, 7250
p: 03 6334 9588
e: info@trevallyngrocer.com
w: www.trevallyngrocer.com
Open: 8.00am - 7.00pm Monday - Friday
       8.00am - 6.00pm Sat, Sun & public holidays

tasmanian scallops 182
boerewors sausage 184

186 VAN DIEMAN BREWING
Will Tatchell
537 White Hills Road White Hills, TAS, 7258
p: 03 6391 9035
e: info@vandiemanbrewing.com.au
w: www.vandiemanbrewing.com.au

slow cooked pork hock 188
short cut beef ribs 190

195 VELO WINES
Mary and Michael Wilson
755 West Tamar Highway Legana, TAS, 7277
p: 03 6330 3677
e: info@velowines.com.au
w: www.velowines.com.au

roasted venison medallions 196
pizza de fruits de mere 198

WESTHAVEN DAIRY
89 Talbot Road South Launceston, TAS, 7249
p: 03 6343 1559
e: info@westhavendairy.com.au
w: www.westhavendairy.com.au
Open: 9.00am - 5.00pm Monday - Friday

palak paneer   204

roasted beetroot + chèvre salad   206

YE OLDE GREENGROCER
248 Charles Street Launceston TAS 7250
p: 03 6334 1456
Open: 8.30am - 6.30pm Monday-Friday
          8.30am - 2.00pm Saturday

smoky mushroom melange   218

pumpkin + baby spinach salad   220

thank you

to all the amazing providores and producers who have joined us in this project. Not only for believing in our concept and trusting us to make this book, but for their ongoing dedication to producing the best food and wine possible and for making the Tamar Valley a culinary destination that we can all be proud of.

index

tamar valley pantry

A

aioli, garlic 50
apples
   lees orchard 107
   pink lady apple custard tart 108
apricot chutney 100

B

Bailey, John T. 7, 14
balsamic syrup 48, 226
basil pesto 48, 226
bbq quail 56
beef
   char grilled veal rib eye 154
   chicken and beef stock 224
   landfall farm fresh 90
   oyster blade steak tagliata 92
   rosevears waterfront tavern 150
   short cut beef ribs 190
   thai beef salad 64
beer
   short cut beef ribs 190
   slow cooked pork hock 64
   van dieman brewing 186
beetroot
   roasted beetroot + chèvre salad 206
   roasted venison medallions 196
berries
   bilambil berry farm 21
   blueberry clafoutis 22
   blueberry + pink grapefruit sorbet 24
   hillwood farmgate 66
   strawberry flambe 70
   strawberry millefeuille 68
   warm strawberry salad 102
   white chocolate brownie 38
bilambil berry farm 21

Blewett, Danielle 8
blueberry clafoutis 22
blueberry + pink grapefruit sorbet 24
blue eye cod romesco 44
boerewors sausage 184
bread
   chick pea + vegetable curry 136
   hot smoked ocean trout on rye 124
   manubread 122
   sweet fruit brioche pudding 126
bridestowe lavender estates 26

C

char grilled veal rib eye 154
cheese
   chèvre tart 118
   free range egg omelette 116
   palak paneer 204
   roasted beetroot + chèvre salad 206
   three cheese fondue 84
   westhaven dairy 202
cheese fondue 84
chèvre tart 118
chicken
   chicken and beef stock 224
   chicken + pistachio terrine 100
   chicken stock 225
   lavender chicken 28
chicken and beef stock 224
chicken + pistachio terrine 100
chicken stock 225
chick pea + vegetable curry 136
chilli oil 227
chocolate
   chocolate genoese sponge 36
   chocolate + orange fudge 176
   chocolate torte 34
   cocobean chocolate 32

warm pear en croute 110
white chocolate brownie 38
chocolate genoese sponge 36
chocolate + orange fudge 176
chocolate torte 34
chorizo sausage linguine 132
cocobean chocolate 32
coffee crème brulée 144
coffee granita 146
coffee parfait 142
coffee shortbread 146
cook's notes 222
coronea grove olives 41
crème patisserie 228
crispy pork belly 166
crystallized pistachios 78
curry
  chick pea + vegetable curry 136
  palak paneer 204

D

duck
  duck confit 62
  potted duck + truffle jelly 158
duck confit 62

F

fish stock 225
four springs produce 46
free range egg omelette 116

G

garlic
  four springs produce 46
  garlic oil 227
  roasted purple garlic aioli 50
garlic oil 227
goaty hill wines 55

H

hare
  seared wild hare's loin 174
harvest farmers' market 60
herb oil 227
hillwood farmgate 66
honey
  chocolate + orange fudge 176
  honey + pistachio fudge 78
  honey tasmania 75
  lavender + honey icecream 30
  prickly box honey panna cotta 76
  warm pear en croute 110
honey + pistachio fudge 78
honey tasmania 75
hot smoked ocean trout on rye 124
hot smoked salmon risotto 130

J

josef chromy wines 83

K

kitchen essentials 224
Kuruvita, Philip 7, 13

L

lamb
  lamb primal rump roast 168
  landfall farm fresh 90
  pulled lamb noisette 94
lamb primal rump roast 168
landfall farm fresh 90
lavender chicken 28
lavender + honey icecream 30
leaning church vineyard 98
lees orchard 107
lilydale larder 114

M

manubread 122
mushrooms
  free range egg omelette 116
  seared wild hare's loin 174
  smoky mushroom mélange 218
mussel broth 58
mussels
  mussel broth 58
  pizza de fruits de mere 198

N

nigel's gourmet on tamar 128

O

olive oil
  blue eye cod romesco 44
  coronea grove olives 41
  salmon + fennel carpaccio 42
orange + star anise sauce 36
organic 21, 180, 217
oyster blade steak tagliata 92

P

palak paneer 204
pears
  lees orchard 107
  warm pear en croute 110
pepperberry
  seared wild hare's loin 174
pink lady apple custard tart 108
pizza de fruits de mere 198
poached blue eye cod 212
poppy seeds
  chick pea + vegetable curry 136
  seared tuna tataki 138

index continued

pork
   crispy pork belly 166
   slow cooked pork hock 188

potatoes
   poached blue eye cod 212
   pulled lamb noisette 94
   roasted purple garlic aioli 50
   roasted venison medallions 196
   short cut beef ribs 190

poultry
   bbq quail 56
   chicken + pistachio terrine 100
   duck confit 62
   lavender chicken 28
   potted duck + truffle jelly 158

prickly box honey panna cotta 76
pulled lamb noisette 94
pumpkin + baby spinach salad 220

R

rabbit cassoulet 86
rhubarb
   bbq quail 56
   rhubarb compote 76
rhubarb compote 76
ritual coffee 140
roasted beetroot + chèvre salad 206
roasted purple garlic aioli 50
roasted venison medallions 196
rosevears waterfront tavern 150

S

saffron
   poached blue eye cod 212
salmon + fennel carpaccio 42
seafood
   blue eye cod romesco 44
   fish stock 225

   hot smoked ocean trout on rye 130.
   hot smoked salmon risotto 130
   mussel broth 58
   pizza de fruits de mere 198
   poached blue eye cod 212
   salmon + fennel carpaccio 42
   seared tuna tataki 138
   smoked fish kedgeree 214
   tasmanian scallops 182
   wild fish 210

seared tuna tataki 138
seared wild hare's loin 174
shortcrust pastry 228
short cut beef ribs 190
sloe gin cheesecake 176
slow cooked pork hock 188
smoked fish kedgeree 214
smoky mushroom mélange 218
spinach
   chèvre tart 118
   free range egg omelette 116
   palak paneer 204
   pumpkin + baby spinach salad 220
strawberry flambe 70
strawberry millefeuille 70
suppliers listing 230
sweet fruit brioche pudding 126

T

tamar valley truffles 156
tasmanian hotel and catering supplies 164
tasmanian poppy seeds 136
tasmanian scallops 182
tasmanian wallaby fillets 152
thai beef salad 64
the mill providore and gallery 172
three cheese fondue 84
tomato + fennel tart 48

trevallyn grocer 180
truffle consommé en surprise 160
truffles
   potted duck + truffle jelly 158
   tamar valley truffles 156
   truffle consommé en surprise 160
tuile biscuits 228

V

van dieman brewing 186
vegetable stock 226
vélo wines 195

W

walnuts
   roasted beetroot + chèvre salad 206
warm pear en croute 110
warm strawberry salad 102
wasabi
   seared tuna tataki 138
   tasmanian scallops 182
westhaven dairy 202
white chocolate brownie 38
wild fish 210
wine
   goaty hill wines 55
   josef chromy wines 83
   leaning church vineyard 98
   vélo wines 195

Y

ye olde green grocer 217